The Mirror Of Helen

The Kaphtu Trilogy: Book Three

by

Richard Purtill

ISBN: 1-4140-5595-1 (e-book)
ISBN: 1-4140-5594-3 (Paperback)

This book is printed on acid free paper.

1st Books - rev. 02/27/04

This book is dedicated to

Lilia Castle
who combines
Beauty,
Wisdom
and a
Noble Heart

Original edition published by DAW Books

Cover art by Don Matitz

Thanks to:

Gord Wilson
Don Maitz
Lucy Davis
Ron Bowles

For more about the Kaphtu Trilogy
and other works by Richard Purtill
Visit our official website at
http://alivingdog.com

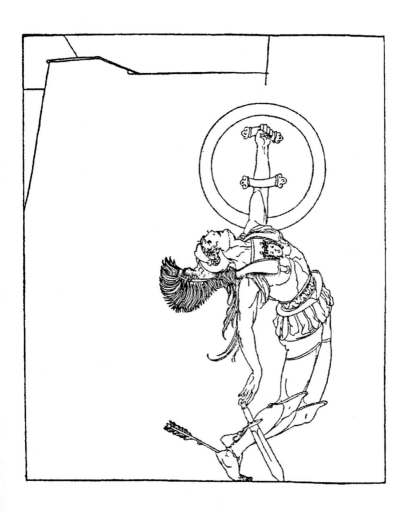

PROLOGUE IN SPARTA:

Theseus

We would never have done it if the Spartans didn't all but ignore the sea. The only fertile part of their rocky land is a small river basin, hemmed in by mountains. Those to the east are high and those to the west are even higher. North is a little better, and to the south there are hills and a rocky bar in the river. From there to the sea the land is marshy and unhealthy. So we could creep up the river, which they call Eurotas, seeing hardly anyone on shore, all the way up to the hills, marking from the heights the easiest routes for approaching the city and escaping from it. Then we waited for nightfall.

The approach to the city was the hardest part of the whole business, creeping along through the fields in mud up to our backsides, trying to avoid setting off too many farm dogs. Luckily the palace was on the edge of the city, near the river. We arrived there just before dawn. I dispatched half our force to steal what small boats they could and put holes in the bottoms of any they couldn't steal. Then Pirithous and I cleaned ourselves up as much as we could: it was essential that we look like visiting nobles for long enough to get into the palace.

We hid in a clump of reeds near the river until the palace was awake. Night assaults sound well, but a fortified palace is closed up tight at night, and the sentries have nothing to do but watch. In the morning there are tasks to do: the guard is changed and the old guard is tired, the new men half awake. People bustle about on various errands and guardsmen are likely to be asked to turn to various tasks;

1

bringing in firewood, opening shutters. They are glad enough to do such jobs for a chance to laugh with the palace maids and perhaps steal an embrace behind a door.

When Pirithous and I strolled in the great gate, we found just the disorganization we expected. Seeing us on foot, the guards naturally supposed that we had stayed with some noble in the city and come unseasonably early to pay our respects at the king's house. We were ushered into the Great Hall while messengers were sent to summon someone of rank to greet us. Luckily we were not offered refreshment: I wanted to incur no guest ties. Of course no one of importance in the palace was prepared for visitors at that hour.

As soon as we were alone Pirithous said in a low voice, "If I remember right, the women's quarters are in that direction...." As he pointed we heard the music of flutes: some ceremony was going forward, probably in a small courtyard off the women's quarters. This sounded promising and Pirithous and I strolled toward the flutes, trying to seem casual: it would be far easier to explain our presence outdoors than if we were found in the women's quarters.

The ceremony was some sort of ritual dance, probably invoking blessings at the beginning of the new day. The celebrant was a young girl, probably not much older than eight or ten. She moved through the dance with a grace worthy of a goddess and she herself was the loveliest thing I had ever seen: golden hair, ivory skin; face of a beautiful child who would be an even more beautiful woman. She was perfectly beautiful and somehow you knew that she had been a beautiful baby and would be completely beautiful at every stage of her life.

When the dance was over she approached us with

complete poise; she might have been a great queen greeting distinguished ambassadors. "Blessings," she said. "I am the king's eldest daughter. My father and brothers are away, and my mother and sister are ill with the river-fever. If you come in friendship I greet you in friendship...." It was some sort of ritual greeting: I interrupted her before she said anything which would put us under some guest obligation.

"We do not come in friendship, princess. I am Theseus of Athens, an enemy of this House."

The priestesses who had been playing the flutes for the dance squealed and would have run, but Pirithous cut off their retreat, his hand on his sword. They stopped, trembling, then the girl looked at us with grave dignity. "What is your errand here. King Theseus?" she asked in a tone she might have used for polite conversation with an honored guest.

"Your father and his allies threaten my lands," I said. "I need hostages for their good behavior."

She smiled faintly. "It's lucky the twins aren't here: you'd never take them with you alive. I shouldn't think you'd want to take Mother and Clytemnestra, they were throwing up all night. That seems to leave me."

I looked into her eyes which were a deep blue. "You should be enough," I said. Any father with a daughter like this would probably do anything to keep her safe. Aside from anything else, her beauty when she was grown would attract every eligible male in the Danaan lands and beyond: her father would have his pick of sons-in-law and the alliances that they would bring with them.

She shrugged ever so slighty. "I don't suppose that I can stop you from taking me. Can I bring some of my things? My chest is up in my room there." She pointed to a window which overlooked the courtyard.

Pirithous grinned. "Give me a leg up," he said. I laced my fingers together and heaved him up: he caught the sill and hauled himself into the room. In a moment he appeared with a small wooden chest, painted in red and blue. He lowered it as far as he could bend and I caught it.

"There's a cloak on the bed," the girl said calmly. Pirithous turned and found it, then lowered himself from the window and dropped lightly to the ground, the cloak over his shoulders. He handed it to the girl with a bow and she inclined her head gravely.

She turned her remarkable eyes on me and asked, "Will you kill anyone who tries to stop you?"

I nodded. "If I have to, princess. War is war."

She looked thoughtful. "Some of the guards are kind," she said. "And I don't suppose they could stop you anyway." She pointed to a small corridor off the courtyard. "There's a barred gate which will take us outside the walls," she said. One of the flute-players made a little sound of protest and the girl turned to her. "Say farewell to my family, Merope. I don't think they'll harm me, they want me as a hostage. I don't suppose it's any use telling you not to give the alarm."

"Wait here," I said. In the corridor we had come through there was a tapestry: one of those things women spend years making on a big loom. I made the women lie on it and rolled them into a bundle, which I tied with a sash I took from one of them. Eventually they'd work loose or be discovered, but it would give us time. "Cover your hair with that cloak," I told the girl, "and show us the gate." She obeyed and walked with a dancer's grace to the gate, watching with interest as we unbarred it and peered out. There was nothing in sight but a few geese scratching in the dust. We set off at a brisk walk for the river. My men rose up out of the shrubbery as we approached, and formed a protective cordon around us: if I had that palace that shrubbery would have been cut down: it provided much too good a cover.

"Wait," said the girl. She took off her sandals and kilted up her skirt and then followed us down the riverbank to where the first boats were hidden in the reeds.

"Enough boats?" I asked the man in charge.

"Just barely," he said. "If she's all you're bringing we'll be all right." The girl climbed into the boat like one who was used to small boats and sat waiting, composed.

"Both of us," I told Pirithous, "if we don't get through with this boat it won't matter." He nodded and took his place in the boat; normally, of course, we would have traveled in separate boats so if one of us was lost the other could lead. This was a fishing boat and smelled of fish, but the sweeps worked easily in the well-oiled leather oarlocks, and it held two of our men as well as Pirithous, the girl and myself. We moved out into the current and signed to the man to stop rowing. Other stolen boats ahead of us launched out into the current at intervals before us and behind us. Too many of course to be inconspicuous, but we had to keep together if it came to a fight.

For a few minutes we kept silent, then we heard shouts from the shore. I hoped it was only someone who saw his boat stolen rather than someone who had missed the princess. "Row for your lives," I told the two men.

Pirithous brought his short curved bow out from under the seat and began stringing it. "They'll head for that rocky bar if they have any sense," he said conversationally. "It would be a fool's game chasing us along the banks."

I nodded. "Probably," I said. "But archers could do

5

Richard Purtill

us some harm at several narrow places with high ground." I turned to the girl. "If they shoot arrows at us, let them get a good look at you and then get in the bottom of the boat. They won't shoot at you on purpose but arrows don't always go where they're aimed."

She nodded and said with an eagerness which somehow reminded me of how young she was, "Have you been in many, many battles? Is it exciting to be in a battle?"

I smiled at her and said, "Well, many. Yes, battles can be exciting if you're fighting in them, or watching from a safe distance, but they're not much fun for a noncombatant caught in the middle of one. Just hope that we can outrun your father's men and don't have to fight."

The girl looked at me with open curiosity and asked, "Is it true that your wife is a Cretan princess. King Theseus? Is she beautiful?"

I grinned at her and said, "Yes, she's beautiful. Dark and fiery, not golden like you. The two of you would make quite a pair. She's the daughter of Minos, the last King of Crete, just as you are King Tyndareus's daughter.

To my surprise she shook her head with an odd definiteness. "Oh, I'm not Tyndareus's daughter. My mother, the Lady Leda, was visited by Zeus while Tyndareus was away fighting in one of his wars. Tyndareus knows I'm not his, but I'm not sure he believes that Zeus is my father." She shrugged and said no more, but her indifference to what King Tyndareus thought was very evident. I looked at the girl appraisingly. Even wrapped in the cloak with her hair windblown she looked like a young princess: the sun had given her skin a faint golden tan and her deep blue eyes sparkled with life.

"You don't seem too downcast about being

kidnapped," I said.

She grinned a gamin grin which humanized her perfection for a moment. "No one ever laughs in our palace," she said, "And we live like poor people, especially when the king is home. He thinks it sets an example to his people."

There was a sort of delicate irony in her last words, and I realized suddenly that behind that childish face was a mind far from childish. A sudden suspicion crossed my mind. "How sick were your mother and sister, really?" I asked.

She smiled faintly and said, "Mother would have done nothing but weep but Clytemnestra would have caused you a lot of trouble. She's a very determined girl." I looked at Pirithous and he laughed out loud.

I grinned reluctantly but said as sternly as I could, "All very well but we didn't raid a hostile kingdom to give you an outing, my girl. We need hostages to keep the Danaan kingdoms from raiding Athens."

She nodded with that curiously composed air she had and said, "Oh, I think I'll do. I'm my mother's eldest daughter and the kingdom goes with my hand. Tyndareus and his Danaans conquered the land but they won't hold it without the marriage tie with my mother's people. To the Old People it doesn't matter who my father was so long as I'm my mother's daughter. But they're not like your Cretans: they won't stand for a brother-sister marriage. Since Tyndareus can't marry me to one of his sons he's made a bargain with Atreus; one of us is to marry Atreus's oldest son, Agamemnon, and the other is promised to the younger son, Menelaus. At least Menelaus isn't as much of a fool and bully as his brother, Agamemnon."

Her distaste for the match Tyndareus had planned for her was quite evident. Too bad the girl wasn't older and I unmarried: Sparta would not be a negligible dowry. How old was this child, anyway? My son Hypolytus was only five; could I hold on to this girl until he was of marriageable age? Hypolytus could not inherit Crete; that went through the female line. If I had a son by Ph'dare should the throne of Athens go to him or to Hypolytus? Well, plenty of time to think of that. "Not even the gods know all the future holds," I said, half in response to my thoughts, but she took it as a response to what she had said about her planned marriage. She shrugged. "Sometimes you think you are running from your fate and you are only running toward it," she said. "But you can try."

The trip down river was not bad; we were fired on by archers from the banks twice, and once they tried to force us under a high bank where men were waiting to fling rocks down and sink the boats. But Pirithous, who is canny about such things, had ordered the men who stole the boats to look for things to act as shields: we had everything from wickerwork hurdles from the fields to an old door from a farmer's shed. Huddling under these, we escaped damage from the archers until the current took us downstream out of range.

We saw the dust from chariots on the road, though, where it came close to the river at one point, and knew that men would be waiting for us at the rocky bar where we would have to abandon the boats. I ordered us ashore at a bend just before the bar and formed us into two groups, with most of our archers in the group behind. The first group formed a hollow square around the girl hostage and set forward at a trot: every moment our enemies had to organize themselves could hurt us.

We rounded the bend to find the Spartan troops still

somewhat in disarray, as I had hoped, but they formed up fairly smartly into a double line barring our way up to the hills beyond which our ship lay. I looked up into the hills and saw the flash of a bronze mirror; a signal which told me that the men I had left with the ship were in position. Then I waved my men forward at a walk, scanning the line of Spartans for their leaders. An armored man with a spear in his hand stepped forward: his shield was on his arm and his helmet on his head. A wiser man would have parleyed with us with his shield on his back, his helmet off and a herald's staff in his hand: at the close of the parley we would have had to wait for him to arm himself or show ourselves lacking in honor. While he armed, his men could have set themselves to attack first or brace for our attack.

The man who stepped forward said harshly, "Give us the Lady Helen unharmed and we'll grant you a quick death."

I spoke to him without slowing or stopping my steady walk toward him: I wanted the distance between us closed as much as possible. "If you fight us the girl may be hurt," I said.

The man sneered. "To Hades with her! She went with you willingly instead of raising the alarm; the little bitch can take her chances."

He must have seen something in my eyes, because he raised his shield and poised his spear. I drew my sword with my left hand: in my right I had the iron club I had taken from the man who had bent my nose with it. Pirithous murmured to the girl, "Get behind me and stay close: hold on to my belt."

The Spartan leader threw his spear but I was already too close for a good throw: a quick duck and it went over my shoulder. I brought the club up low and fast: I hit the inside edge of his shield and knocked it away from his body. He was quick: his sword was already in his hand and he cut at me with it. I parried his sword with mine, and as my blade bounced from his I used the motion to make a cut at his upper arm. My sword sliced into his biceps and blood spurted. At the shock his arms fell to his sides, leaving his head unprotected; my club came up and smashed his face in.

The next man kept his spear and thrust at me with it. I parried with my sword in my left hand, feinted with my club to get his shield to his left, changed the motion of the club to a transverse swing which smashed his right shoulder, and put my sword in his throat as he fell back. Another man came at me, cautiously, his shield held forward and a sword in his hand: if he had carried a spear he must have hurled it. His left leg was too far forward: I kicked the bottom of his shield viciously, driving it into his shin. He fell forward: likely his leg was broken. A quick swing of my club and his head was broken too.

A movement to my right made me whirl, but it was a man falling, with a black Lapith arrow in his back. Our archers from the ship were walking down the hill shooting arrows at the unprotected backs of the Spartans. The archers from the group that had come down the river with me kept firing arrows at every target which offered itself: if a Spartan turned to shield himself from the archers in back an arrow from the front got him. The flight of the arrows sounded like a swarm of angry bees.

In a few moments the seemingly invulnerable line of bronze-clad warriors had melted away. Where their lines had met the river, bodies were lying in the water, sending long threads of red down the stream. Carrion birds were already beginning to circle above.

Some of my men who had attacked the line with me were on the ground dead or dying. They were all tough, dirty fighters but the armor, spears and shields of the Spartans had given them an advantage. Without our archers and the ambush from behind we would have gone down before the Spartans. Pirithous had a cut on his neck and a Spartan spear in his hand. He had probably caught it in midair with that juggler's dexterity of his. He had stood his ground with the girl hostage behind him, but had probably done his share of damage despite that.

I snapped out orders to get the Spartan chariots, cut the traces and stampede the horses, then went to the girl; "Lady Helen" the man I had killed first had called her. She was deathly pale and her animation had gone leaving her still lovely, but like a statue of gold and ivory. "No more blood, little one," I said as gently as could. "This lot must have used every chariot that could be mustered. Before men can get here by foot we'll be over the hills and on our way downstream in our ship. They'll never catch us now."

She looked at me, her eyes bright with unshed tears: she couldn't keep a little quiver out of her voice as she said, "I've never seen a man killed before."

I put a hand on her shoulder and guided her gently up the slope away from the bodies, toward the ship that would take her from her homeland.

Much blood has been shed for Helen of Sparta since, but that was the first.

BOOK ONE

Alceme

BOOK ONE: Alceme

Chapter One

APHIDNA

I met Helen of Sparta for the first time because Menesthius was worried about Theseus. Menesthius had always been the worrier, the responsible second in command in the little group of Athenians who had been taken to Kaphfu to leap the bulls in the great Dance in honor of the Sea God. When Theseus killed Astariano, the monstrous son of the wife of M'nos, and took the Athenian Dancers back to Athens, Menesthius easily slipped into the position of being his second in command, ruling Athens for Theseus while the warrior-king was away on his many adventures. In fact, things were a great deal more peaceful and orderly in Athens when Theseus was away, I had been told. I could well believe it, though I myself had lived for many years in Karia on the Asian mainland as the wife of a sea trader I had met and married in Kaphtu. Now my husband was dead and I was back in Athens for a time.

I had heard rumors about the growing infatuation of Theseus for the Spartan princess he had captured as a hostage, and the growing rage of his wife, Ph'dare the Kaphtui princess. She was openly flirting with Hippolytus, the son of Theseus by an earlier marriage, and the situation was as full of potential trouble as a wasps' nest is of wasps.

The capture of Helen had been a way of getting a hold over Sparta and her Argive allies, who had raided Kaphtu and threatened Athens. But even as a child Helen had begun to acquire a reputation for fabulous beauty, and I suspected that this was as much an attraction for Theseus as Helen's value as a hostage. Theseus had hidden Helen away in a small city in the interior of Attika and put his own mother, Aethra, in charge of the girl. Since then, Theseus had been unusually dutiful in his visits to his mother and tales were beginning to be whispered about Theseus and Helen. If Ph'dare's behavior with Hippolytus was a response to these rumors it would not be surprising to anyone who knew Ph'dare.

I could see plenty of possible trouble for Athens in all this, and I found that despite my years of living in Kaphtu and then in Karia, I still cared a great deal what happened to Athens. I decided to talk with Menesthius about it and after I overcame his first reluctance to discuss the problem he poured out his worries, very similar to mine. "There's no end to the trouble it might cause," he told me. "Old Tyndareus, the Spartan king, wasn't ill-pleased to have Helen stolen away. For one thing, she's not his: Zeus fathered her on Leda, Tyndareus's wife. For another, I suspect that Tyndareus had secretly promised her to the sons of half the neighboring kings, and was just as glad to have her taken away: otherwise he'd be accused of oath-breaking whoever he gave her to. But if it gets about that Theseus is seducing the girl, then Tyndareus will have to do something: his sons will force him to even if he's reluctant. So there would be war with Sparta."

"Is Theseus seducing her?" I asked bluntly. Menesthius shook his head, but his face was troubled. "I don't think so, not yet at any rate, but he shows signs of becoming obsessed with her. Ph'dare certainly suspects that something is going on and she's playing the devil with young Hippolytus in revenge. If Ph'dare leaves Theseus or goads him into killing her, Kaphtu may revolt. Theseus has neglected it anyway and that might be the final insult that leads to rebellion. But Kaphtu can't defend itself against the Argive raiders any longer: they've become too dependent on Athens."

"All this because an aging man has lost his head over a girl," I said in disgust. Menesthius agreed dejectedly. "And that's not all," he sighed. "If anything happens to Hippolytus because of this we may have trouble with the Amazons, Hippolyta was their queen and high priestess. Her son has some special significance for the Amazons that I don't pretend to understand: I don't think that any male knows much about their religion or customs."

I shrugged. "The Amazons live half the world away," I said. "I'm not much worried about them. But a war with Sparta would draw in the whole Argolid and it could be the end of Athens. And I don't relish more Argive raids on Kaphtu either: they did enough damage after the Great Wave. I wish I could do something."

Menesthius looked at me with sudden hope. "Perhaps you could," he said slowly. "I know where Helen is hidden, but I don't dare go there myself and I couldn't find out much if I did. But if you made some excuse to stop there on a journey supposedly to somewhere else you might find out a good deal. Helen is rather like you were as a girl. That is...."

I laughed at his embarrassed expression. "If you mean that she's a selfish, self-centered little bitch who enjoys her power over men, you can say so," I told him. "I know what I was like, and I know that I was luckier than I deserved when I decided to marry N'suto. All right, Menesthius, I'll go have a look at this paragon and tell you my judgment of the situation, for all the good it will do."

He shrugged. "It's always better to know," he said. "Sometimes you can do something, and even if you can't it's better to worry over real danger than a myriad of imaginary ones. Thank you, Alceme. I'll start making arrangements for the journey immediately." I had sometimes wondered what might have happened if I had stayed in Kaphtu or returned to Athens. Part of my question was being answered now: I found that the life of a woman in Athens was intolerably restricted after the freedom I had enjoyed as a Dancer in Kaphtu and a merchant's wife in Karia. For my journey to a shrine in the north which was to give me an excuse to stop at Helen's hiding place, I had to travel in a closed litter with an armed guard and a steward "in charge" of me, as if a woman of my years and experience needed to be charge of any man. Ph'dare and her favorites had a little more freedom than most Athenian women, but even their lives were hedged in by all sorts of restraints that a Kaphtui or Karian woman would have laughed at. If I had returned to Athens after being a Dancer in Kaphtu I would soon have left it again, I was sure.

We were very plausibly benighted near the little village of Aphidna and quite naturally my steward knocked on the outer door of the only house of consequence in the village to ask shelter for the noble lady in his charge. Keen-eyed guards, far too many and too good for a little country manor house like this, scrutinized us carefully and sent my entourage to spend the night in the village. I and the steward alone were admitted, and ushered into the room that did duty as the Great Hall. Two women sat by the circular hearth and the steward retired with murmured words of respect, leaving us alone.

The older woman was a dark-haired lady of the Old People with the remnants of great beauty: she reminded me of my mother-in-law, Riamare. The younger woman was still hardly more than a girl. Her hair was golden, her eyes a deep blue, and she carried herself with the assurance of an Olympian. Rightly so: she was the most beautiful woman I had ever seen. But her eyes were bright with suspicion and her face was hostile: she was looking at me as if she wanted to kill me.

The reason for Helen's hostility soon became apparent. "An Athenian lady conveniently benighted," she sneered, "Another spy of Ph'dare's!"

Obviously any attempt at evasion would only feed her suspicions: nothing I could do would convince her that I was really benighted there accidentally. I drew myself up and looked her in the eye. "I am Alceme, the Leaper," I said, "Lady of the House of N'suto, First Councillor of Karia. If I were spying for anyone it would not be Ph'dare."

The older woman's eyes widened and she made a sign with her fingers. For once I was grateful to Riamare who had insisted on initiating me into Mysteries which I would not have meddled with on my own. I gave the countersign and the older woman gave an inclination of her head, equal to equal. "I am Aethra, Lady of Troezen and this is my ward, Helen of Sparta," she said. "Welcome to this house." She turned to the golden-haired girl. "You owe this lady an apology, Helen," she told her.

But Helen was already looking at me wide-eyed. "Are you...were you...really a Leaper?" she faltered. "I'm so sorry...I think I've heard your name, now I stop to think. Leapers and Amazons are the only women he really respects, and I've always... please forgive me." It was obvious enough who "he" was, and if I had been forced to leave the house at that moment I would have known the essentials of the situation: Helen had fallen into a girlish infatuation for the man who had kidnapped her, and he could probably do whatever he wanted with her. Knowing as much about Theseus as I did, I had very little confidence in his ability to resist the opportunities which the situation gave him. I studied the girl's flawless features with more compassion now: Helen was a victim in this affair, not a villain.

There was something rather appealing about this dazzling girl in her penitent mood and I smiled at her. "Don't worry," I told her, "I had my own problems with Ph'dare, long ago: I don't blame you for scorning someone you thought was a spy of hers." I turned to Aethra. "In fact if Ph'dare knows where you are...."

Aethra smiled rather unpleasantly. "One of her creatures traced us here, but no message got through to Ph'dare, I assure you," she said. Helen looked troubled and I wondered just what had been the fate of Ph'dare's spy. "But please, Lady Alceme," she continued. "Draw a chair up to the fire and tell us of your travels." I seated myself and gave them a suitably cut version of my journey. I said nothing of my Olympian friends and implied that my husband's death had turned my mind to old times and that I was visiting Menesthius and T'ne mainly because of our past association in the Dance.

Aethra relaxed completely. "That explains how you came here, if the people with you belong to Menesthius," she told me. "My son trusts him absolutely and he is one of the few who know of this house, and no doubt he gave your steward directions to stop here in case of necessity. Now that you are here why not stay with us a few days? My ward and

I would be grateful for your company." Helen seconded her eagerly; she longed to ply me with questions about the Dance. Feeling a little ashamed of my duplicity, I allowed myself to be persuaded. I was genuinely tired and soon retired to bed, well satisfied with the first moves in my game.

In the morning there was a knock on my door and. Helen herself entered, bearing fruit, hearthcakes and steaming herb tea. She served me with charming diffidence, but eagerly accepted my invitation to perch on my bed and chat.

"You have something on your face to make you look older, don't you?" she asked, ingeniously. She had keen eyes: my makeup as an older woman had aroused no comment from T'ne or Menesthius.

I smiled at Helen and said, "Yes, it's safer to look like an old woman when you travel. Not many people notice: I've been practicing this makeup for a long time. I'll take it off if you like and show you how it's done." For some reason she was eager for me to do just that, and brought me what I needed to restore my normal appearance. I shook out my hair and lay back against my pillows, rather flattered by the admiration in her eyes.

"I thought that under that stuff you were beautiful," she said.

I shook my head with a smile. "Not compared to you," I told her.

She made a little face and said, "Thank the gods for that. You're quite lovely enough to know what it's like to be only a Face and a Form, to be looked at like a work of art with no one caring about the woman behind the face." I thought of myself as a girl, conscious of dazzled looks on men's faces and the sour looks on women's faces as I sauntered by, deliberately flaunting my beauty in my brief Dancer's kilt. Had I ever felt like that?

Some memories returned and I said slowly, "Yes, I know what you mean. But I was lucky enough to have some good friends, and to find a man who thought of more than my body. And the bull doesn't care what you look like." Helen nodded eagerly. "Yes, I envy you that so much," she said, "to have found something real to do, something that doesn't depend on how you look. And the only man I've found who looks beyond my face is...." I could finish that sentence for her, I thought: "is old enough to be my father"; "...is Ph'dare's husband";... "is Theseus, King of Athens."

I looked into Helen's eyes. "Are you sure he sees beyond your face?" I asked softly. "How do you ever know?" she asked with a trace of bitterness. "How did you know?" A dozen answers crowded into my mind, memories of N'suto's tenderness when I was nine months pregnant, of facing together the illnesses of our children, the ruins of some trading ventures, the death of a child I had lost. Then a simple test occurred to me. "Can you laugh at things together?" I asked.

"Yes," said Helen proudly. "Laugh together and walk together and talk together. And ride and run together too: he forgot once and said I ought to have been a boy." I sighed and gave up for the time being: Theseus was either being very clever or he had a genuine affection for this beautiful child. I had wanted to run and ride and do the other things boys did when I was a girl and any adult who had encouraged me would have won my heart easily. If the adult had been a fine looking man who was hero of a hundred adventures I might easily have become as infatuated with him as Helen evidently was with Theseus.

Helen went on with a tinge of bitterness. "If you've never known any Spartan men you're lucky: none of them would talk to me as if I were a human being or do anything with me that didn't involve some approach to love-making. Last time he was here. The...the man I'm speaking of, spent most of his time teaching me to use a bow. I managed to shoot a water bird and we grilled it over a fire of sticks and shared it." Clever Theseus, I thought, to know the kind of wooing that would capture the girl's heart. I felt a sudden conviction that it must be wooing: a man like Theseus would always have that in his mind with a girl as beautiful as Helen. I wondered how much time Theseus had spent with his own daughter, Akama.

Helen would gladly have talked more of Theseus, but I thought it best to turn the conversation. "Would you like to see how I make myself look older?" I asked.

She agreed at once and observed me with a curious intensity, then asked hesitantly, "Could you teach me how to do it? I've had a thought sometimes that I could pretend to be ill for a while, then make myself ugly and see how... people...treated me."

I hid a smile: every beautiful woman dreams of finding a man who will love her for herself, even if she lost her looks. Of course the dream usually includes the scene where you show the man that you haven't lost your beauty after all. All of us want to keep the fruit and eat it too. I cast an eye over Helen's face and frowned. "It would be hard," I said slowly. "To look older I color in my wrinkles to make them more obvious, but you have no wrinkles. I darken the hollows in my face to look bony and gaunt, but you have no hollows. Just painting the surface of your skin won't do.... Well, let's have a try."

Helen's face was enough like mine so that I could use tricks I'd learned would work for me. I spoiled the delicate arch of her eyebrows, made her lower lip look pendulous, and then got to work on the lines and hollows. I had to work on where the wrinkles might start in ten years, and where the hollows might come if she grew thin. Then I had to shade and tone until it all looked natural. I stepped back and must have made an involuntary grimace, for Helen said anxiously, "Didn't it work?"

I forced a smile. "It worked too well," I said. "I feel as if I'd destroyed a work of art. My mirror is over on the table there. Use the silver side: the copper side always flatters you. When you get to my age you try to make yourself look as well in the silver side as you do in the copper."

Helen was taking a long look at herself in the mirror. She spoke slowly. "It's almost frightening," she said. "I've gotten into the habit of thinking of my face as a curse, as something that stands between me and other people. But to meet others like this... I'd feel...defenseless...."

"It will wash off," I told her.

She nodded. "Yes," she said, "but the memory won't. It's easy to wish that people didn't stare at you and admire you, but if they didn't...I'm not sure that I'd like being... ordinary...as much as I thought I would."

"I'm glad you've realized that, Helen," said a voice from behind us. "Your face is your destiny." I turned and saw what seemed to be an old servant woman. But there was something about the quiet certainty in her voice that reminded me of the Olympians I had known. The appearance could very well be an illusion. I looked at the woman—or goddess—closely and peeping out from the hem of her dress

I saw a small, exquisitely shaped foot in a golden sandal.

"Bright Lady," I murmured and gave her the Kaphtui gesture of respect: my hand carried to my brow as if to shade my eyes from the sun. If this Olympian woman let out her full glory I would need to shade my eyes in truth and not just in symbolic gesture.

She did drop her disguise, but kept her brightness to a tolerable level, a faint golden glow which bathed her skin in light. Even had Helen not been disguised by makeup her beauty would have seemed faded and ordinary beside the superhuman beauty of the goddess. It was a face you could stand and gaze at, lost in delight. Her mouth was full and sensual and there was a spark of malicious amusement in her eyes. This could only be Aphrodite. They called her the laughter-loving goddess, but her laughter was not always kind.

"Ah yes," she said, her words tinged with mockery. "The little friend of our new virgin goddess. I had my eye on you for awhile, Alceme, but you were taken off to leap bulls while I was busy elsewhere. It might have been amusing to play you off against some of the others. But you didn't have the potential that Helen does."

I didn't quite dare to say so but I was very glad of that. I remembered Britomartis telling Ariadne and me, before Ariadne had become a goddess herself, that some of the Olympians treated mortals almost as playthings. Better to be ugly than to attract the attention of this capricious goddess and be a pawn in her games. From what Britomartis had told me I knew that Aphrodite caused trouble among the Olympians with her love affairs with gods and mortals. I suspected that when that amusement palled she chose some mortal woman and used her to play out games of vicarious love and power. I shuddered inwardly and kept my mouth closed.

Aphrodite's eyes were on Helen now...with a sort of calculation that reminded me, madly enough, of N'suto planning out a new trading venture. "I have plans for you, girl," she said. "Before long you'll be going back to Sparta...."

"No," said Helen in a low, tense voice that was somehow more expressive of her utter loathing of the idea than an outcry would have been. "Never!"

The Olympian lifted a lovely eyebrow. "Oh, you won't stay there," she said. "But it's essential that you go back for a while." Helen's face was white under the makeup, bringing out the artificiality of the lines and patches. "They'll marry me to Agamemnon!" she cried.

Aphrodite shook her head. "No," she said with an undertone of amusement in her voice. "Agamemnon was fobbed off with Clytemnestra when Theseus stole you away. Menelaus is the favored claimant now."

Helen looked bewildered. "The red-haired boy? I hardly remember him. At least he can't be as bad as Agamemnon. But I won't marry him! I won't marry anyone except...."

The goddess's eyes began to sparkle with irritation and I nerved myself to intervene. "Helen, you can't bring anything but ruin to Theseus. Revolt in Crete if he casts aside Ph'dare to marry you, war with Sparta even if he marries you and all the more if he makes love to you and doesn't marry you. I know what Theseus is like from friends who know him well. He loves Athens, he loves being King of Athens. Even if he would give up everything for you, and I don't think he would, do you think you could make him happy if having you meant losing Athens?"

Helen looked stunned and I felt unhappy with myself for joining with Aphrodite to ruin her romantic dreams. I consoled myself with the thought that every word I had said was true; better for her to be told this than to learn it by bitter experience. Besides, Aphrodite was not the kind of Olympian it was safe to defy. She might flare up and kill Helen or hurt her badly. But it wrung my heart when Helen looked around her with tears in her eyes and said brokenly, "Sparta!"

The seeming collapse of her resistance pleased Aphrodite and she said with a little cajoling purr in her voice "Come, Helen, don't be a fool. You'll no longer be a child to be disciplined and ignored: you'll be the next Queen of Sparta and you'll be treated as such. And you'll dazzle them all: just wait until you see the effect you have on men now you're grown up." Helen's eyes became dreamy: the Olympian was using her power to control Helen's mind, I was sure. "Go back to your room," Aphrodite told her, "I'll come to you later." Helen left the room like a sleepwalker and I felt again that I had betrayed her somehow.

Aphrodite turned to me and I braced myself, but she seemed pleased with me. "You said the right thing at the right time," she said. "If she had determined to defy me I might have had to hurt her. Luckily she doesn't know her full powers yet. She's a daughter of Zeus even though her mother is mortal."

"Can she..." I began, and fell silent.

"Live in Olympus?" said Aphrodite. "Perhaps. And Theseus can't: another reason to stop that affair. You know more about the Olympians than is altogether safe for a mortal, but you seem discreet. Farewell, Alceme!" And with an enigmatic smile Aphrodite vanished.

Chapter Two

THE TWINS

On our return journey we had followed the coast for much of the day and were just about to swing inland for Athens, when the steward approached me, agitation in his low urgent tones, though he kept up a good picture of normality in his face and voice. "Lady Alceme," he said, "the peasants have told me that there are black ships beached on the coast near here that crept in around the islands to avoid being observed by Athenian lookouts. And there is a group of armed men on the road ahead, Argives by the look of them."

"I will speak to them," I said with as much confidence as I could muster. I hoped that I had not faced an angry goddess only to be killed or kidnapped by some little wandering group of raiders. As I came in sight of the armed men, however, I saw that they looked more like the regular troops of some Argive kingdom than like pirates. There seemed to be two men in command: young men in richly decorated armor who looked like brothers but seemed to be about the same age. One of them came up to me and saluted me courteously enough but his face was grim.

"I am sorry to interfere with your journey, noble Lady," he said, "but now that you have seen us we cannot allow you to go on to Athens and warn Theseus." I faced him with as confident an air as I could manage. "Theseus has little need of a warning from me," I said. "Athens patrols her coasts well: you'll be spotted long before you get anywhere near the city. Whatever hope of gain or glory brought you here you've little chance for it."

The young man lost his air of assurance: "Lady, I do

not know what to say," he said in a shaken tone. "My brother Castor and I have sworn to rescue our sister Helen: we risked everything on this raid. If what you say is true, there's our only chance gone...."

My mind was racing. These must be Pollux and Castor, the twin brothers whom Helen had spoken of in tones of exasperated affection; when she had left Sparta they had been boys, up to every kind of mischief. Behind this raid I could see the meddling hand of Aphrodite who wanted Helen back in Sparta to further her schemes. Athens was well defended but a determined raid could do great damage. "Helen is not in Athens," I said slowly. "You have my word on that: I have spoken to her, not long ago." There was skepticism on the face of Pollux and I said with a smile, "She told me how you put the rooster under the priest's robe for the dawn sacrifice. ..."

The two brothers looked at each other and exchanged boyish grins. "She's spoken to Helen all right," said Castor. "We never got caught on that one, but slyboots sister Helen knew." He turned to me earnestly and said, "Lady, we mean no harm to Athens, we'll even leave Theseus unpunished if we can get Helen back without fighting him. Tell us where to find our sister, so that we can bring her home."

I sighed. What I was about to do would certainly be regarded by Theseus as a betrayal, and perhaps by others too, but I thought that it would be best for Theseus, for Helen herself and certainly for Athens if I yielded to Castor's plea. "Get back to your ships and pretend to return home," I told them. "Helen is at Aphidna, a little town in the north not far from Marathon, where Theseus killed the bull. She won't want to go with you: she's infatuated with Theseus, but make your prayers to Aphrodite and you may have Olympian help."

The brothers looked hard at me and then at each other, seeming to communicate without words for a moment. "All right," said Pollux slowly, "we'll trust you: we have no real choice. We thank you. Lady, and whatever one of the Immortals who led us to you. May we know your name?"

I didn't know whether to feel like a savior to Athens or a traitor to my city as I said, "I am Alceme, daughter of Akademos the Councillor." Pollux nodded gravely. "If war ever does come between Athens and Sparta, your father's lands will be sacred to us," he said. I nodded solemnly but it meant little to me: my father's lands had passed to cousins I scarcely knew.

They made a good enough show of reluctant retreat and I watched the Spartans march back to their ship with very mixed emotions. They would strike Aphidna quick and hard, and there would be little bloodshed. Before Theseus could take any effective action they would be at sea, with a good chance of a clear run to a friendly port on the Argolid. Very likely they would be safe in Sparta before news even got to Theseus of the raid. Lives would be saved. Both Helen and Theseus would be happier in the long run, but I still felt that I had betrayed someone who had trusted me, no matter how good my reasons. I remembered, the tone in which Helen had said, "Sparta." I sighed again and turned my face toward Athens.

What happened when we returned to Athens is no part of Helen's story, nor am I over-fond of remembering it. Whether she was enraged by Theseus's preoccupation with Helen or merely bored and malicious, Ph'dare continued her pursuit of Hippolytus until something snapped in one of them. Her story was that he tried to rape her, but I think it just as likely that she tried to seduce him and he had repulsed her so strongly that she made the accusation in revenge. A scorned woman is deadlier than a serpent as the saying goes.

Be that as it may, her accusation made Theseus fly into a rage with Hippolytus and chase him from Athens with a drawn sword in his hand. When it looked as if Hippolytus would escape in a ship he had taken, Theseus called on his father, Poseidon, the god of the sea, and Poseidon sent a great monster like a bull from the sea to destroy the ship and Hippolytus. Whether in remorse, or in fear of her husband's revenge if he found the truth, Ph'dare hanged herself. Theseus wept for her, but I think he was not sorry to be free of a wife he had married chiefly for her kingdom.

He was grim enough for a while, more because of Hippolytus than because of Ph'dare, I felt. The city itself was in a strange mood; Athenians were shocked by the loss of their queen and of the prince who had been regarded as heir to the throne. The confidence that Athenians had always had in themselves and their city seemed to be faltering, at least for a time, and I was more confident that I had done the right thing in diverting Helen's brothers from the city.

When I was with Theseus though, I still had misgivings. He talked of his plans to make Athens even greater and balance the growing Argive power and I wondered how much he counted on an alliance with Sparta by marriage with Helen. With Theseus it was always hard to tell how much he wanted a woman for herself and how much he wanted what she could bring him. He took every opportunity to bring me into prominence with the Athenian people and he often mentioned the name of my father, Akademos, who had been a counselor to the Athenian kings. I thought wryly that I was probably the second string to his bow if Helen failed him;

just as he had prudently courted Ph'dare as well as Ariadne when he had gone to Kaphtu as a Dancer.

The peaceful days came to an end when grim-faced, travel-worn messengers arrived from the north with news of the raid on Aphidna. Theseus soon sent for me and his face was hostile as he said, "I've been told that you met some Argive raiders on the way here from Eleusis and frightened them off. Or did you buy them off with information?"

I faced him as steadily as I could: his own earlier efforts to make me popular would stand in the way of any drastic vengeance now. "I told them where Helen was," I said bluntly. "Athens can't stand another war now, and Aphrodite wanted her back in Sparta: she would have accomplished that one way or another, without caring much what happened to Athens." Theseus scowled. "Curse the Olympians and their meddling!" he growled. "Those misbegotten twins will have Helen back in Sparta by now and my mother with her." That was a shock: it was natural enough for the brothers to take Aethra hostage in return for the kidnapping of Helen by Theseus, but that was a consequence I had left out of my reckoning.

Theseus fixed his eyes on me with a curious intentness. "Was it only for Athens that you got Helen out of the way?" he asked. The moment of decision was on me: if I told Theseus that I had gotten rid of Helen to eliminate a rival for his affections I might quickly find myself Queen of Athens. Did I want that? Ought I to accept that destiny whether I wanted it or not? I looked at the face of Theseus, filled with an urgent demand for affection, for reassurance. I simply did not have within me to give what would satisfy that demand. "Only for Athens," I said, looking into the gray-green eyes of Theseus. His face took on a closed, withdrawn look: I knew he would not ask me again and I felt an irrational pang of loss.

"I decide what is for the good of Athens," he said harshly. "It seems that I must go to Sparta and claim what is mine." I opened my mouth to protest and closed it again: I had lost the only argument that would have counted with him. I bowed my head and left the room, wondering if I should have married Theseus to prevent this insane raid which would surely fail and would give Sparta an excuse to invade Athens in return.

I was soon aware of a change in the mood of Athens as well as in the mood of Theseus. There was no popular enthusiasm at all for a war with Sparta over a captured princess no Athenian had ever seen. Theseus was not cynical enough to claim that the raid was to recover his mother, and indeed poor Aethra seemed almost forgotten. Remembering the affection that had seemed to exist between Helen and Aethra, I consoled myself with the thought that Helen would do everything she could to lighten Aethra's lot.

The mood of the people was growing increasingly ugly, as the full implications of war with Sparta became clear: the remaining able-bodied men sent off to risk life and limb in a distant land, the constant vigilance which would be necessary against counterattacks even if a raid was successful. Furthermore, Athens might have to fight the whole Argolid for Helen: news had reached Athens that Tyndareus was playing his old game of half-promising Helen's hand to every princeling of a country whose support might strengthen his reign.

At last things came to a head: a delegation of the most prominent Athenians, craftsmen and large farmers as well as nobles, came to the King's House and demanded an audience with Theseus. Normally women would been barred from such assembly but I still retained enough prestige as a former Dancer to make my way in without any overt challenge, though I got hostile looks from some of the men. The leader of the delegation, an old noble who was universally respected, did not mince words. "King Theseus, we have sent for Lord Menesthius from the north," he said. "Give up this mad idea of war with Sparta or we will put him on the throne of Athens in your place!"

Chapter Three

THE SUITORS

For a moment I thought that Theseus would call his guards and have them imprisoned or hurled from the Hill. His eyes blazed and his nostrils flared; he almost leapt up from his chair of state, and I could feel the fatal commands trembling on his lips. But he must have realized the futility of fighting the whole of Athens, as represented by these men, for after the first flare of rage his shoulders slumped over slightly and resignation replaced the anger in his eyes. "So long as I am king, I expect my commands to be obeyed," he said with dignity. "I cannot let you face me down and continue to have the name of king without the power. But if you will not follow me freely I will not whip you into a battle which you have no stomach for. Let Menesthius rule. He has been faithful to me: he will be faithful to Athens."

The delegation was, I think, amazed and a little frightened at their own success. In the old days it would have been Theseus who faced them down, shamed them if he could not have inspired them. But the lust for power that had brought him to the thrones of Athens and Kaphtu was, at least for now, stilled. He had let Kaphtu go and now he was letting go his hold on Athens. He voiced the reason himself as he said quietly, "My son is dead. My wife is dead. I am weary. Give me a ship and a crew of volunteers. I go voyaging: this time I will not return."

The old nobleman spoke with awkward gentleness. "Lord Theseus, if you raided Sparta, even with a single ship, Athens would be embroiled...." Theseus shook his head with a bitter smile. "That is not my plan, you old fox," he said to the noble. "That dream is over: without the power of Athens

35

to bully Tyndareus I cannot hope to get Helen. It was a forlorn enough hope even if Athens had been behind me: the Argive princes are clustering around Helen like flies around a honeypot. Hope that they quarrel with each other enough to weaken the Argive power; once Sparta is allied with the Argives you will have trouble from the Peloponessos."

They would miss Theseus if it came to war with the Argives and they knew it as well as he. If he had wanted to, Theseus could probably have played on their fears and ended with them promising their support to him if he took back the throne. But I think he was half glad to be unable to pursue Helen. As he had said, that dream was over. Theseus turned to me with an ironic smile. "Will you see me off at the port. Lady?" he asked. He might be planning to kidnap me, for vengeance or for other reasons, but I could not humiliate him by a refusal to trust him, after what had just happened.

"Of course. Lord Theseus," I said. As news spread of what happened crowds began to form, milling around confused and uncertain. The Athenians were weary of war, but they were remembering their pride in their adventurer-king too. They wanted him to go, they wanted him to stay: he could easily have inspired them to follow him anywhere. But he went straight to Phaleron, where it seemed that every sailor and fighting man in Athens was assembled, begging to volunteer for his crew. Theseus passed through the crowd, here and there clapping some tried companion on the shoulder. In each case the man broke into a delighted grin, though he would be following Theseus to exile and perhaps to death.

I caught up to him as he arrived at the side of the ship he had chosen, a good sized, well found trading and raiding vessel. "No, Lysias," he was saying to a man, "stay here in

Athens: your children need you. And Menesthius will need some men who know one end of a spear from the other." He turned to the men he had chosen. "I've picked bachelors and widowers," he told them, "for we won't be coming back to Athens. If any of you has a girl he can't leave, drop out now and let another take your place. If the seas don't suck us down we may voyage till we reach the Happy Isles!"

They gave a cheer and Theseus turned to me and said in a low tone, "I am going to Skyros where I have a kinsman I can trust. You may hear that Theseus died in some accident there. The old fox was right, Athens will be blamed for what Theseus does, so the name of Theseus had best be dropped into the sea. But don't believe all you hear; perhaps you and I will meet again."

I smiled at him. "Whether or not we do, I will be glad to think that you are still in the world, Theseus. My good wishes go with you and—forgive me. For everything."

Theseus shook his head and grinned, "I have drunk the cup of kingship, time to go on to new things. As for Helen, it may be just as well not to become entangled in her destiny; I think it will be a bloody one. The only thing I regret in our meeting is that which you did not have to give me. But the world is wide and there is always something—and someone—new." He grinned again, embraced me with a hug that made my bones crack and ran aboard the ship as lightly as a boy. I was not the only one who watched his sail until it was lost on the horizon.

If anyone but Menesthius had taken over the throne of Athens there might have been trouble of one kind or another, but the Athenians were so used to Menesthius ruling while Theseus was away that the change was hardly noticeable. Menesthius now had the name of king as well as the task, and the Athenians found life more predictable, though less exciting, without their adventurer-king. Things in time grew so quiet that I was beginning to think of my home and my children in Karia, but that was when the envoy from Sparta came.

He was more courteous than most Spartans, but under the smooth surface there was the Danaan arrogance that I had grown unused to, living in Karia. I had taken to wearing my old woman makeup again to avoid questions as to how I had grown miraculously younger since my previous visit, and the eyes of the envoy flicked over my face without interest, but he bowed ceremoniously when I came into the throne room in answer to a summons from Menesthius.

"The Lady Alceme, daughter of Akademos the Councillor?" he asked. I nodded and he went on, "The Princess Helen asks that you visit her in Sparta: she and her brothers will make you most welcome. We hope that she will decide between her suitors soon and there will be great feasting at her wedding." His tone said as clearly as words that an old crone like myself would be out of place at such a feast.

"What of King Tyndareus?" I asked, more amused than offended by his courteous words and insulting tone.

The man shook his head and said in tones that seemed to hold some genuine sadness, "The King is failing; if Princess Helen will only make her choice her husband will be our new king."

I looked at Menesthius, who drew me aside and said quietly, "I have little fear of trouble with Sparta now that Helen and the husband she chooses will rule: she is not one to seek vengeance, I think, and she is likely to choose a husband whom she can bend to her will. But I may be wrong, and if you refuse to go the Spartans could choose to take offense. Do as you wish, Alceme, but if you are not too disinclined to go I would like well to hear what you make of the Spartan court and of the man Helen chooses."

I had been growing restless in Athens and knew that despite my desire to see my children I would be equally restless in Karia: Helen's friendly gesture in inviting me had aroused my sleeping guilt about betraying her hiding place to her brothers, and I wanted also to be sure that Aethra was not too unhappy in Sparta. "Oh, I'll go," I told Menesthius, "for curiosity if nothing else. But I won't stay long. Sparta is no country for a woman, at least not a woman like me."

That was abundantly clear both in the Spartan ship that bore the envoy and myself back to Sparta and in Sparta itself. The city of the Spartan kings was not a seaport: most of the Spartan coast was marshy and unhealthy and the city was separated from the coast by a low range of mountains. Aboard the ship I was kept in as much seclusion as was possible, and when we sailed up the river as far as the mountain range I was immediately clapped into a closed litter for the journey over the mountains to the city. I would much rather have walked over the pass and the seclusion on the ship had been especially galling since I was used to the freedom of sailing with N'suto on our own ships.

Once at the palace I was ushered with some show of deference to the women's quarters and found Helen sitting placidly in an interior courtyard, with Aethra beside her. She rose and embraced me, then stood back to look at me, smiling faintly as she observed my makeup as an old woman. Helen had matured since I saw her last, and her beauty was now almost supernatural: she rivaled Aphrodite herself. No wonder every princeling of a country friendly with Sparta was clustering around her.

Helen linked her arm with mine and as we talked we strolled along the path which surrounded the center of the courtyard. After a few polite inquiries about my voyage her voice changed and she said with tension in her voice, "We've heard rumors here that Theseus fell or was pushed from a high place in Skyros; do you know the truth of it?"

The same rumors had been heard in Athens. In fact the unfortunate kinsman of Theseus who was lord of Skyros was already being accused by malicious tongues of murdering Theseus for some fabulous treasure he had hidden in his ship. The ship had disappeared and I knew what that meant, but so far I had told no one of what Theseus had confided in me at the dock in Phaleron. But Helen had a right to know. "Theseus is off roving," I told her, "and thought it wise to leave his name behind. But tell no one this." I hesitated, then added, "You are not likely to see him again."

Helen gave a little sigh. "I know, but I'm glad he's alive nevertheless. He stole me from this very courtyard, do you know that? That's why I love to sit here and... remember. Perhaps I shouldn't: the trouble with knowing a man like Theseus is that he spoils other men for you. Most of my suitors seem like unlicked pups compared to him. But you'll see them yourself, that's one reason I asked you to come."

There was something that had to be settled between us: I slipped my arm from hers and faced her. "Helen, I told the twins where you were," I said. "I had good reasons, but nevertheless, I ask you to forgive me."

She smiled and shook her head. "Aphrodite told me that she would never let me marry Theseus," she said simply. "I'm only glad no more blood was shed in carrying out her will. Aethra is angrier than I am, even though she came with me of her own choice. The boys didn't know that she was the mother of Theseus until she told them so herself. May I tell her about Theseus? She doesn't believe he's dead, but she'll still be glad to hear your news."

I agreed, of course, and Aethra thanked me smoothly enough but there was a hostile spark deep in her dark eyes. Was it her own captivity she resented, or my frustrating her son's plans? I pretended to believe her pretense but turned with relief back to Helen, who seemed genuinely glad to see me.

Over the next days I became Helen's principal companion, especially when she was meeting with her suitors, for now that Aethra's identity was known, she was an embarrassing reminder of Helen's kidnapping. The Argive princes, who wanted her for her beauty and for the throne she could bring them, would have preferred to forget that kidnapping. For any girl without Helen's advantages that kidnapping would have ended any hope of marriage: Spartan girls were jealously guarded until they were handed over to their bridegrooms. I did not think that Helen and Theseus had been lovers: she might still be a virgin. But no Danaan male would believe that, I thought, and most of the suitors tried to pretend that her adventures with Theseus had not happened rather than admit that the peerless bride they were seeking might be "damaged goods."

There were two suitors who caught my attention especially. One was a red-haired young man with a nose a little too large for his youthful face, Menelaus, the second son of Atreus the Argive king. I remembered that Aphrodite had spoken of him as the suitor favored by Tyndareus, but he was now being overshadowed by suitors with more maturity and address. His eyes followed Helen with doglike devotion whenever they were in the same room, but he said little, and often blushed at some real or fancied bit of awkwardness which he committed.

The other suitor who impressed me was an older man: Odysseus, the king of the little island kingdom of Ithaka. He was a stocky man whose legs were a little too short for his finely muscled torso, but he was very quick and agile. His eyes, though, were what impressed me most: they were alight with devious intelligence and took in every detail of everything he saw. He saw through my old woman makeup at a glance and when I watched him maneuvering and bamboozling his fellow suitors he saw that I knew what he was doing and gave me a cool ironic smile of understood complicity. His voice was deep and soft and you could understand when you heard him the old phrases about people who could charm the birds from the trees and the fish from the sea.

It was one of his maneuvers which brought the situation with the suitors to a head. They were already growing snappish with each other and any suitor who was favored with a smile from Helen or a few moments' conversation got black looks from his fellows. By gradual persuasion and clever rhetoric, Odysseus got all of the suitors to swear an oath that all of them would support and defend whichever suitor Helen eventually chose. I thought he hoped that he would be that suitor, but I did not think that he was much bedazzled by Helen's beauty. It was Sparta he wanted and the chance for greatness that rule of a larger kingdom would give him. Even as island kingdoms go, Ithaka is small, poor and rocky.

I soon knew that Odysseus, despite his schemes, had

no real chance with Helen: she was a little afraid of that deep and devious mind of his, I think. But I had no idea who she did favor until the day the suitors were summoned to hear her choice.

Ordinarily this would have been announced by Tyndareus, or since he was weak and ill, by another male relative: but Helen had a way of getting men to ignore rules and customs when it suited her. She stood before the assembly, outwardly demure and submissive, but with that inward self-possession which I was beginning to recognize as the key to her character. Whoever she gave her hand to, Helen would always be her own woman.

She smiled serenely at her suitors and exploded her thunderbolt in her lovely melodious voice. "In choosing a husband," she said demurely, "I am of course guided by the wishes and promises of my revered father, who has promised my hand to the brother of my dear sister's husband. His choice, and of course mine, is Menelaus, prince of the Argives." Menelaus paled and swayed as he stood, so great was his surprise. The other suitors murmured, and if it were not for their oath, might have protested aloud. But a little smile played about the lips of Odysseus as if instead of losing the prize he had won some deep and devious game.

Chapter Four
THE BRIDE

It was not a popular choice: there were discontented mutterings from the suitors and after a few moments a big bearlike man with an untidy shock of dark hair raised his voice and bawled, "To Hades with that! Old Tyndareus half promised her to half the Argolid; there's no more reason to honor one of his promises than another. I say we choose among ourselves who shall have the prize. If we set up contests in all the manly arts...." There was renewed angry talk among the suitors: obviously in many kinds of athletic contests the huge protestor would have an advantage over more normally proportioned men.

A smaller man with a self-important air called, "It should be settled by lot, I've always said so. It's the only fair way...."

"My friends!" said a deep voice from the side of the crowd, and Odysseus walked slowly to the front of the room, near where Helen stood, with a faint smile, apparently unmoved by all this. "My friends," repeated Odysseus, "have you forgotten the dreadful oaths you took to respect Helen's choice and defend the man she chose from all attacks? Ajax, you are a great warrior, but if you or any man breaks his oath, he will face the rest of us united against him, as well as the anger of the gods. You are behaving like a man who risks more than he should on a throw of the dice and when he loses wants to fight the other players. Helen is, as you can see, a dutiful daughter and will be a faithful wife: once she has given her word she is not likely to change her mind for all your blustering."

Helen's face was hard to read, but I thought that she

was not pleased by this inference, and I was sure that she had not missed the note of irony in the last words of Odysseus. She smiled at him with an edge of malice and said with honeyed sweetness, "Perhaps you have less interest in the outcome than my other suitors, Odysseus. I understand that my father has promised you the hand of my cousin, Penelope."

Odysseus was apparently unperturbed by these words, though they caused renewed murmuring among the other suitors. "Why, it is true enough, Lady, that your father promised me Penelope's hand as a consolation if your choice did not fall on me, and since I am only the ruler of a little island kingdom, an older man with little to recommend me to a lady's favor, I did not really expect your choice to fall on me. Menelaus is young, and will not lose his vigor while you yourself are still young; everyone knows the dangers of that!"

There were sniggers from the suitors, for the story of a young queen who bears a child when her husband seems past the age of siring was a familiar one: some of the suitors were seeking their fortunes by marrying Helen because their putative fathers looked on them with just that kind of suspicion. That such things happened was the not surprising result of the Danaan preference for young, docile wives.

Odysseus went on smoothly, "All the kings of the Peloponnesus look with respect on Agamemnon, king of men, the brother of Menelaus who is the ruler of mighty Argos. With Argos and Sparta in the hands of two such brothers as Agamemnon and Menelaus, it will be a bold man who will threaten the peace of the Danaan lands." The implicit threat in his words was not lost on the suitors: Argos would be an uncomfortable neighbor for any suitor who got the throne of Sparta in spite of the brother of Agamemnon.

A coaxing note came into the deep voice of Odysseus as he concluded his little oration, "Come, my friends, let us take our disappointment like men, and give our hearty congratulations to this fine young man who is the successful suitor." He took Menelaus by the hand and led him to Helen's side. Menelaus was flushed and confused, but he gave Odysseus a look of humble gratitude and clasped his hand as if Odysseus had saved his life; as perhaps he had. Helen had no choice but to play up and greet Menelaus with charming modesty, while the suitors raised a rather halfhearted cheer.

"Now let those who cannot wait to... marry...follow my example and console themselves with the lovely ladies of Sparta," said Odysseus, and there was ribald laughter and catcalls from the suitors. Stewards appeared with wine cups and began mixing wine and water in large vessels, and the assembly began to turn into a rowdy party. Helen withdrew as soon as she could, and I was following her example when I became aware of Odysseus at my elbow.

"What was Helen playing at, do you know. Lady Alceme?" said his deep voice in my ear. I turned and faced him. His eyes were those of a man who really saw what he was looking at, and I was sure that he was not deceived by my makeup. I felt a faint unreasonable uneasiness at his knowing my name, as if it gave him some power over me.

I shrugged and answered him, hearing the faint drawl in my voice which sounds insolent but which I know is a sign that I am on the defensive, "I wouldn't know," I told him. "She doesn't confide in me. I doubt if she confides in anyone. What is it to you, King of Ithaka? What are you playing at?"

He chuckled, quite unoffended. "Only keeping the peace. Lady Alceme. I'm a peaceful man. I had the idea that

Helen wouldn't have minded a fight among the suitors, for some reason. Well, she's got Menelaus now and she could do a lot worse: he could be a good husband to her if he'd stand up to her. But I'm not sure that he will: he's enchanted by her like everyone else."

I raised my eyebrows, rather intrigued by this devious, charming man. "Everyone except Odysseus?" I drawled.

He gave a deep chuckle of genuine amusement. "I don't cry for the moon, Lady Alceme, even though I can admire its beauty," he said. "That one doesn't want a husband who can see through her."

I laughed despite myself. "Few women do," I replied.

He grinned. "Penelope doesn't mind," he said. "She's honest clear through and has nothing to hide. But I'd guess that most intelligent women don't really respect a man they can bamboozle."

I smiled a little sadly, remembering a husband who had understood me very well and loved me very well. Then something about what he'd said struck me. "You don't think Helen is intelligent then?" I asked. He shrugged. "She's never needed to be," he said, "with those looks. I think with a woman like Helen it's very difficult to see below the surface. Perhaps until she grows up a bit there isn't much there below the surface. Of course with some women what's below the surface can be very different from the appearance." He grinned at me conspiratorially and I had to laugh at his impudence.

I was curious enough about the woman Odysseus had chosen to try to meet Penelope. That was easy enough: I had already seen her around the palace but she had been too quiet and unobtrusive to make me notice her much. She was a dark, rather plain girl who reminded me a little of T'ne. Next time I met her in the women's quarters I said something conventional about her betrothal to Odysseus. Immediately her face lit up and she became much more attractive.

"Helen was a fool not to choose him," she said with quiet certainty. "He's much the bravest and cleverest man among the suitors. I'm not sure why she chose Menelaus, unless it was to humble the others. Of course he's so besotted with her that she can do pretty much as she likes with him; perhaps that's the attraction. But she'll despise him unless he stands up to her."

I smiled at her. "That's just what Odysseus said," I told her.

Her answering smile lit up her plain face and for a moment she was almost beautiful. "He's very clever about people, isn't he?" she said. "I think he understands women about as well as any man can. He knew that I—liked him—I wouldn't dare to tell him." I went away from that talk curiously impressed with Penelope as well as with Odysseus. No doubt once he carried her off to his rocky little island kingdom no one would ever hear of either of them again, but I knew that I would remember them both.

Whatever Helen had intended by her choice of Menelaus, the intervention of Odysseus meant that their marriage went smoothly. The festivities were decorous.

an unkind person might have called them stingy. The Spartans are not known for liberality or for geniality. A conventional few days after the wedding I went to take my leave of Helen and wish her happy. She was, if possible, lovelier than ever and there was a certain complacency in her expression which made me smile inwardly; she had evidently enjoyed her wedding night.

I tried to hint at this as delicately as possible and she smiled her small secretive smile. "I chose well in that respect," she said frankly. "Menelaus didn't confuse me with a citadel to be taken by a storm. He was—rather sweet. But sweetness won't get him far with the Spartans, or with my brothers. Well, time enough to worry about that when the king dies or relinquishes the throne to us. For now the only job Menelaus has is to make me happy."

"Are you happy, Helen?" I asked with a little pang of conscience. After all, if it were not for me Helen might not have been here.

She gave a little shrug and said, "It's not as bad as I thought it would be, back in Aphidna. Tyndareus seems to have...shrunk: even if he weren't old and ill he wouldn't be the ogre my memory made him. It's good in a way to come back here where I grew up, hear the Spartan twang in the people's speech, see so many things unchanged. It...won't be forever you know. Aphrodite has plans she won't tell me about."

I had forgotten that, and it gave an added poignancy to my parting from Helen: I was leaving her not to a settled future but one which was at the mercy of the whims of an Olympian whose laughter was often unkind. Whenever I have heard of Helen since, I remember her eyes as she said, "Aphrodite has plans...."

BOOK TWO

M'pha

BOOK TWO: M'pha

Chapter One
THE AMAZON

I remember the day the Amazon came. It was soon after they buried Lord Hector's body and the City was still in mourning, but the arrival of Penthesileia and her contingent of Amazon warriors threw the population into a tumult of rejoicing. The City was like that in these days, swept alternately by despair and hope. A defeat on the fields of battle and there would be long faces everywhere, then would come a rumor of new allies or of growing disaffection in the Argive camp, and everyone would be foolishly optimistic; even the slaves and tradespeople swaggering and boasting about "unconquerable Ilium." I wake up in the night sometimes after a vivid dream of those days and feel again the trapped, closed-in feeling that every inhabitant of the City felt after nine long years of siege.

We were in prison, but it was an open prison. The Argives were too few in number to blockade the city: when not actually engaged in battle they mostly kept to their camp on the shore by their ships, impossible to dislodge but at times seeming more a nuisance than a real threat. The King sometimes called them "that nest of pirates down on the shore" and it was very much like living near a stronghold of pirates or bandits who would periodically swoop out of their camp for raids. They raided the neighboring lands as often as they attacked the City: from our neighbors they could get food and wine and captives to serve them. From their attacks on the City they gained only the glory they so often prated of and the slow deadly attrition of our fighting men. Sometimes they stripped the armor from a fallen foe or held a captive City warrior for ransom, but our warriors did the same to them, and both sides came out about equally in that traffic. Man for man they outkilled us, and despite the unconquerable walls of the City we inside those walls felt a fear gnawing more and more at our bellies.

Probably the Argives would have attacked any body of men bearing arms attempting to enter the city, but like all Danaans the Argives despised women and likely Penthesileia could have brought her fighting girls into the city in full battle array without any Argive response. Prudently she made them keep their weapons out of sight and the Argives let her troop of horsewomen enter the Scaean Gate with no more than a few jeers and taunts sent after them from the Argive scouts. But once inside the gate they were met by the King's messengers and stopped at the guardhouse to put on their panoply of war. Then they rode through the city to the King's House in their barbaric splendor.

I watched them coming from the roof of the House: tall women mostly, lean and rangy with big hands and hardbitten faces, javelins and longbows strapped to their backs and jutting up over their shoulders like some strange sort of horns. They rode their shaggy horses bareback, almost as much a part of their mounts as a centaur's human torso is part of the horse body below. Riding before them, as deadly dangerous as any warrior in her troupe, but beautiful as the rosy-fingered dawn, was their leader, Penthesileia.

She was dark, like my people, and proud as any daughter of the Sea Kings. For ten years I had served the most beautiful woman in the world and compared to my Lady, Penthesilea could hardly be called beautiful. I am near kin to the Ariadne of Kaphtu, and compared to the daughter of M'nos this girl was hardly more than the chieftainess of a little barbarian band. Yet there was a beauty and an authority about this Amazon princess which could not be diminished by any comparison. She had the deadly beauty of an arrow or a flung javelin arcing swiftly to its victim, yet she was a girl, straight and sweet and honest. If she had lived in my older, kinder, land I would have welcomed her as a fellow Leaper of the bull.

There was a little choking sound from behind me and I turned to see the mad princess gazing wide-eyed at the Amazon. "What do you see, Cassandra?" I asked, half out of curiosity and half perhaps from kindness for the poor crazed princess who got little but scorn from most folk.

"You won't believe me," she said dully. "Why do you ask?" I could say nothing to this that would not be hurtful, so I stayed silent and after a moment she said in the sing-song voice she used for the "prophecies" which somehow it was impossible to take seriously, "I see two paths for her. In one she is lying bright-faced in an Argive tent, while the Argive lover kisses her hands. In the other she is lying on the ground with dead men in armor lying around her. The same man is kissing her hands, but she is dead and her eyes—her poor eyes...." Cassandra gave a little sob and I tried to comfort her. The vision was typical of her prophecies: likely enough this Amazon girl would fight for the City and likely enough she would die in battle or be raped by the Argives if she was captured. But she was as little likely to be bright-faced in an Argive bed as any Argive was apt to kiss her hands, dead or alive.

"No doubt if you asked her, she'd prefer to be dead than in an Argive's bed," I said drily as I watched the Amazon dismount and stride into the House. "Come, Cassandra, let's go see her greet your Father." There was more calculation than kindness in this, for the mad princess could wander anywhere she pleased and if I were attending her I could go where she went. On my own, I would hardly dare to enter the Great Hall when the King was welcoming important visitors. My blood was as good as that of the royal family but to the folk here I was merely my Lady's serving woman and ranked at best as an upper servant.

Cassandra was biddable enough when not having one of her fits and she led the way to the Great Hall with me in her wake. King Priam was standing beside the hearth in the center of the Great Hall, making a formal speech of welcome. Queen Hecuba sat on her low-backed chair beside him, a small secretive smile on her face. It occurred to me that the queen might have something to do with the presence of the Amazons here in the City: Hecuba was a priestess of the Mother but she had her fingers in many other women's Mysteries. The Amazons worshiped the Virgin Huntress, but the Queen might well have found some way to call on their aid.

The Amazon princess was too well-schooled to reveal her impatience with Priam's flowery phrases, but as soon as he stopped—for breath more than likely—she spoke, simply and directly. "I thank you for your words of welcome. King Priam," she said. "But before you welcome me let me tell you why I am here. I come to be cleansed of blood-guilt." There was a little stir among the courtiers in the hall at this, for the only sort of blood-guilt that would require this sort of cleansing would be guilt for shedding the blood of close kin. It was not uncommon in the Argive kingdoms for one of the many sons of a king to quarrel with and kill one of his brothers or half-brothers and be sent off to cleanse his guilt at the court of some conveniently distant priest-king. Women, I would have thought, would have had more sense, but the Amazons are more like men than women in many ways.

But when the Amazon told her tale it was more of tragedy than of guilt. Penthesileia and her cousin Hippolyte had been hunting in the woods: each had thought she knew the other's position and each had been wrong. Penthesileia had loosed an arrow at a deer but instead had killed Hippolyte, her young cousin who was next in line to the throne of the Amazons. Penthesileia and Hippolyte had been blood sisters: the older girl had been sworn to protect and defend her young cousin: instead she had accidentally killed her.

"I am next in line to the throne," said Penthesileia, unable to keep a slight tremor from her voice, "but it was unthinkable that I should profit by my deed. The Council laid a task on me: to come and offer my service to Priam, King of the City of the fertile plains. If I die defending your city I have given blood for blood: if I do some great deed in the service of your city you may absolve me of blood-guilt and send me back to the land of the Amazons."

I looked at Penthesileia with compassion. Priam needed every spear he could muster: he would be unlikely to send Penthesileia and her followers back home, no matter how bravely they fought, unless the war took a turn very much for the better. Hector had been one of the great warriors of the age, but even he had fallen at last. How many of these Amazons would ever see their native plains or their horse herds again? I wondered if Hecuba, had suggested this "solution" to the Amazon Council and if that accounted for her secretive smile.

Priam stood in thought for a moment, then said with

a slight sing-song in his voice that reminded me unpleasantly of his mad daughter, "This is my judgment. The enemies of this sacred City are not many in number, but they are mighty warriors. Remove from battle one of their leaders and your blood-debt is satisfied: go back absolved to the homeland of the Amazons." Penthesileia bowed her head gravely, but I was hot with indignation on her behalf. One of the Argive leaders indeed! Which one did he expect this slim warrior girl to cut down, wily Odysseus, Diomedes whose war-cry chilled the blood, dread Achilles himself? I slipped away, disgusted, but as I left I heard the Amazon saying gravely, "While I live my Following will fight at my side; if I fall they will carry my bones home. I ask you not to try to keep them here..."

I myself would not trust Priam even that far, as I told my Lady when I poured the whole tale out to her when I attended her bath that evening. Her reaction was unexpected, as it was so often. Behind that exquisite face and form was an acute and devious intelligence and genuine, if somewhat selective benevolence. My Lady would look out for herself first, and after that for those, like myself, who she felt belonged to her. But after she had taken care of herself and her people she would sometimes go to considerable lengths to help those who took her fancy.

I could see that the Amazon girl had captured her interest when she said after a little pause for thought, "Poor creature...Cassandra is probably right, she usually is.... I'd like to talk to this Amazon, M'pha. See if you can arrange it. You probably can; you know everyone and most people like you."

I laughed. "Most people are eager to meet you," I said bluntly. "If only out of curiosity. I shouldn't find it too hard to arrange. But what do you mean about Cassandra? No one takes her seriously."

My Lady raised her exquisite brows and said in a musing tone, "No they don't, do they? It's very curious because she is usually right. And yet people won't listen to her, I rather think that Someone is interfering. A certain sort of Someone." I met her eyes with sudden understanding. We both knew more about the Olympians than was altogether safe for a mortal, though she was in less danger than I, for she herself was half Olympian. However, even my Lady dared not oppose Olympian schemes, at least openly. Any mortal who did that would simply be brushed aside, if not crushed. But Cassandra...? Surely my instinctive disbelief in her "prophecies" was merely common sense...or was it?

My Lady rose from her bath and stood for a moment by the fire, ignoring the towel I held out to her; either her Olympian blood or her consciousness of her own beauty made her indifferent to nudity. "Things are coming to an end, M'pha," she said musingly. "This war has to end soon, one way or the other, and the air is thick with schemes, Olympian schemes as well as mortal. We can't change anything very big, M'pha, but perhaps we can interfere a little around the edges. Anyway, we can try. Bring me that Amazon."

It was easy enough once I found that Priam had asked his son Deiphobus to act as host to Penthesileia. Deiphobus had been infatuated with my mistress ever since his brother had brought her to the City: he would do anything to get into her good graces. A few words to Deiphobus and Penthesileia soon appeared at my Lady's house, puzzled but deferential. The Amazons are far from being barbarians, but the society of the City is almost as ancient, ingrown and complex as that of the Sea-King's court in Kaphtu: she must have found the customs strange enough so that the request to visit the wife of Priam's son and heir was no more puzzling than other things that had happened since her arrival in the City.

She came in a simple dress of white, with the diadem and girdle which showed her to be a priestess of the Huntress. She brought one companion, a lantern-jawed woman who looked as if she would have been comfortable in fighting rig, but whose behavior was seemly enough.

My Lady received her in the hall of our house, with myself and Aethra, her other lady in waiting, in attendance. Penthesileia and her companion were given comfortable chairs and served refreshments: a few pleasantries were exchanged, but when the servants withdrew Penthesileia frowned and said bluntly, "I am honored by your invitation, my Lady, but I don't understand why you wished to speak to me."

My Lady smiled gently but replied with equal bluntness, "King Priam has given you a task. Lady Penthesileia: to eliminate one of the Argive leaders. These men are the greatest warriors who draw breath under the sun. How do you propose to set about it?"

"Why do you want to know?" asked Penthesileia, courteously but not hiding the fact that she thought it none of my Lady's business. "To help you if we can," said my Lady, with her small secret smile. Penthesiliea looked at the three of us, her face impassive, but her companion's face revealed the contempt which Penthesileia's polite words concealed. "I do not quite see how you could do that..." she began.

My Lady's smile grew a little wider. "Why, we are not quite such domestic fowl as we appear, Lady Penthesileia," she said. "Lady Aethra, my elder companion is the mother of King Theseus of Athens, who many hold to have been the greatest warrior of our age. My young friend, M'pha, was a Leaper of bulls in Kaphtu before she became my friend and companion. We three have shared some adventures together that even an Amazon might find a little out of the ordinary."

My Lady lifted her brows a little and her golden voice took on a little more depth and authority as she said quietly, "I am no warrior myself, Penthesileia, but I have known some great warriors, including most of those you will face in battle. I am a daughter of Zeus, Ruler of the Olympians, and I am not without some powers of my own. And I have a right to be interested in what happens in this war if anyone does: they say it is being fought over me. I am Helen of Sparta. Paris brought me to this city, and the Argives are at its gates to take me back."

Chapter Two
THE NET

My Lady Helen was already half a legend even then and the widening of Penthesileia's eyes showed that she was impressed. "I appreciate your interest. Lady Helen..." she began, but my mistress cut in before she could finish. "I have enough blood on my conscience," my Lady said quietly. "I don't want yours too. I know a good deal about Amazons, Penthesileia, from Theseus and from others. You're hit-and-run fighters, archers and horsewomen. When your army besieged Athens, it was defeated: that wasn't your kind of fight and neither is this. The fighting here is mostly hand to hand, with spears and swords; there's very little in the way of tactics or strategy. When the City troops try any kind of formation the Argive leaders break it up like human battering rams. Most of them are big men and some, like Big Ajax, are almost giants."

My Lady eyed Penthesileia keenly. "No doubt you can run down a deer: it's part of the Amazon training. Achilles could do it in full armor. I'm sure that you're good with your javelins and arrows, but Argive armor is good and a warrior like Diomedes can run, jump and move in it so quickly that you'll never have a stationary target. If you fight the Argives their way you'll be dead in a few days at most." Penthesileia kept her composure but you could see that she was shaken. "What can I do then?" she asked.

My lady's beautiful face was thoughtful. "That's what we're here to think about," she said. "If Theseus were here I'm sure he'd find some way. I'd back him against any of them. He had ten times the brains of any of them except Odysseus and he was the quickest man I've ever seen. He could snatch a bird out of the air. He'd study their weaknesses, bide his time and strike when they were vulnerable. But I can't tell you how he'd do it."

I reflected, as I often had, that the only man whom Lady Helen ever praised with that kind of enthusiasm was Theseus, who had kidnapped her when she was scarcely more than a child but won her heart by liking and respecting her.

Penthesileia shook her head doubtfully and said in a voice in which hope warred with despair, "I see that I have less chance even than I thought. You are kind, my Lady, but what can you do.... Perhaps the Mother is taking this way of making me pay for the blood of poor little Hippolyte...."

My Lady gave the delicate little snort of contempt with which she greeted any sign of self-pity. "Nonsense, girl," she said. "Tell me, who rules the Amazons now?"

Penthesileia looked at her in puzzlement. "Why, the Council," she said. "Hippolyte and I were the last two with any sort of claim on the throne and we were only cousins of the royal family. Your Theseus cut off the direct line when he kidnapped our kinswoman. Queen Hippolyta."

Lady Helen shrugged. "You Amazons cut off the line when you killed Hippolyta rather than let her stay with Theseus," she said, "But that's an old quarrel. How many women loyal to the Council were on the hunt with you when Hippolyte was killed? An arrow of yours may have killed her, but who swore that it came from your bow? Was Hippolyte a novice at the hunt, to step in the way of an arrow? Do you shoot when you can't see your target clearly?"

As Lady Helen shot these questions at her, Penthesileia's head lifted, her nostrils flared and her eyes glinted with a dangerous light. "If I thought that..." she began, but her lantern-jawed companion cut in, speaking for the first time. "There were many thought that things were not what they seemed, my Lady," she said, "but as soon as they told you that it was your arrow killed Lady Hippolyte you were mad with grief and couldn't stop accusing yourself."

Lady Helen cut in, with an authority in her voice which made you remember that she was a queen and the daughter of the Olympian King. "Men of war will fight on any pretext or none," she said. "If I were not the reason for this war they would find another. But I do not want your blood shed in this war, child. Be guided by my friends and myself. Use your woman's wits to kill one of the Argive leaders and go home full of glory to claim the throne they tried to steal from you."

Penthesileia was a soldier; she knew real authority even when it was concealed by the soft and lovely body of my mistress. "I will do whatever you tell me, my Lady," she said quietly. "You have given me back something I thought I had lost forever."

Helen turned to Aethra and myself, "I must consult my councillors," she said with a little touch of self-mockery. "Aethra, what would your son have done?"

Aethra knitted her brows, still dark, though age had silvered her hair and stolen all but the last remnants of the great beauty that had been hers. "He would have said that if you cannot fight a man with the usual weapons, you must fight him with weapons he does not expect," she said thoughtfully. "Sciron the bandit battered down swords and spears with his iron club, but Theseus ducked under his club and fought him hand to hand: broke his back with a wrestler's hold. He kept Sciron's club, though, and used it against swords and spears himself at times."

"Weapons that they do not expect, good," said Helen and turned to me. "M'pha, I know that the bull-dance itself is not a fight but the bull-dancers go out and capture a wild bull for their Dance," she said. "How did you subdue the beast, what weapons did you use?" She knew as well as myself, having often asked me for stories of my days as a Dancer, but I knew that this was for Penthesileia's benefit.

"Weapons are forbidden," I told them. "Capturing the bull was a test of courage and skill for the children of the Sea King in the old days, and they were forbidden to use anything but ropes and sticks. Nowadays the old rule is stretched a bit: we use nets to snare the bull and a long forked pole like a fisherman's trident to fend him off."

"A net and a trident, yes," murmured my Lady. "Something could be done with those against a heavily armed man." She turned to Penthesileia. "Have you hunted with a net?" she asked the Amazon. "Can you throw a net to entangle game as hunters do?"

The Amazon nodded, puzzled but intrigued. "Small nets, yes: we use them for rabbits and for fawns we want to keep for sacrifice."

My Lady smiled grimly. "This time," she said, "you will hunt bigger game."

I was sent off to the huts of the hunters to find the biggest and best made nets I could find, then to the fisherfolk to find a trident. Aethra sent for our old servant Phyrgos, who had been one of Theseus's men long ago and was now serving as a captain of the City guard. He came, as instructed, in full fighting gear: bronze helmet with nodding horsehair plume, the heavy shield which could cover his whole body when he crouched behind it, bronze corselet and greaves. His sword hung at his side from a baldric slung over his shoulder and his great spear was in his hand.

"You fought the Amazons of Athens, Phyrgos," said Lady Helen. "How would they do in the war here?"

Phyrgos shook his head, making his helmet plume dance. "Not well, my Queen," he said in his rumbling voice. "Amazons are bonny fighters. They can fire an arrow or javelin as well from a horse as most men can from the ground. If a group of them can ride you down, a foot soldier can be in lots of trouble. But that battlefield out there is full of frustrated archers who can't put an arrow through shields or armor: any horse who stays out there long will be as full of arrows as a sea-urchin of spines. That's why the great lords ride their chariots out to battle and then send the horse and chariot back to their lines quickly. At Athens it was our Lapiths who killed the Amazon horses. But some of the allies here are almost as good as Lapiths with those short double-curved bows."

Phyrgos looked at the two Amazons a little apologetically and went on, "On foot an Amazon fights like a wildcat, but you can't wear bronze armor on a horse, and horseman's armor won't stand up in hand-to-hand fighting with a bronze-clad foot soldier. One to one they wouldn't stand a chance: their weapons can't get through the armor and our weapons have the reach on them. Brave as lions, though. The King was weeping at the way we had to slaughter them to break their siege at Athens and he wasn't the only one." For Phyrgos only one man was "the King," without qualification—Theseus, who had been King of Athens.

My Lady met Penthesileia's dark eyes with her brilliant blue ones. "Theseus wept again when he told me the tale, Penthesileia. That's why I had a great fear for you when you and your companions rode into Ilium so proud and beautiful. You don't belong in that slaughterhouse out there on the plain."

Penthesileia's face was grim. "Perhaps not. Lady Helen, but I am vowed to go there and to kill my man. If you can really help me...."

Lady Helen smiled and said quietly, "Oh, I think we can. Phyrgos, could you kill M'pha here?" She gestured to me where I stood in my old Dancer's kilt, one of the nets I had gotten from the hunters balled in one hand and the trident I had found among the fisher folk in the other.

Phyrgos grinned a little sourly. "I doubt it, my Queen," he said. "I've seen my lady here dance with the bulls and she's as quick and agile as a monkey." The spear had left his hand almost before he finished speaking, but I had seen his muscles tense and it was easy enough to gauge where the spear would come and step aside. I tapped the spear down with my trident to spare the wall hanging and it fell to the floor with a clatter. Phyrgos chuckled. "You see, my Queen?" he said.

"Stalk her with your sword," my Lady directed, and Phyrgos came after me in a warrior's crouch, sword in hand, grinning but no less deadly for that. I maneuvered him into position by making him follow me, then threw my net hard and fast, so that it snapped open over his head and settled around his body. A quick jerk on the cord in my hand which was still attached to the net and Phyrgos overbalanced and fell with a crash of bronze. With a quick move I was standing over his head with the sharp points of the trident poised at his throat. "Peace, enough," he rumbled and I helped him to untangle himself and get to his feet.

"Now try that again when I know what's coming," said Phyrgos with a grin, no worse put out than a Dancer would be who had taken a tumble practicing a new leap. We went at it again and this time it was harder to set him up for the throw but he was no more successful in evading the net, or in keeping on his feet once entangled. The third time, though, he evaded my throw and came at me, grinning, with his sword poised. It was my turn to cry, "Peace, enough." I turned to my lady. "If he could catch me, he could kill me," I told her. "There's no way that I could refold the net with him after me, or fight him off with the trident."

Lady Helen nodded. "A second net would be good," she said, "and something to keep your opponent at a distance in case of need. Not a bow, too awkward. A sling perhaps." She turned to Penthesileia. "Could you do what M'pha did?"

The Amazon nodded slowly. "I'm not as agile as your bull-dancer," she said, "but I've been trained from childhood as a huntress. I can throw the net as well as she did and use a sling too. I think more could be done with that trident than she did. If your man isn't too sore I'd like to try it."

Phyrgos, who was as tough as old leather, grinned assent and the game began again with Penthesileia, her skirt kilted up and her ornaments laid aside, wielding the net and trident. She would never have made a Dancer but she was fleet of foot and her aim had a deadly accuracy. She used the trident more than I had, to feint Phygros's sword and shield out of position. Once when he braced himself and could not be pulled down with the net she used the trident to trip him up.

At last even Phyrgos began to get up a little less lightly and when an involuntary groan escaped him my Lady called a halt. "Thank you, Phyrgos," she said gravely. "Not a word to anyone of this, of course."

He grinned. "Have I ever babbled your secrets, my Queen?" he asked with mock sorrow. Then he took off his helmet and wiped his brow, looking at Penthesileia speculatively. "I'm not as young as I was. Lady," he told her, "but I have more cunning than most of the young ones. If I can't escape that net there are few men who can." He saluted with his sword and sheathed it, then clanked out of the room,

"You have only to pick your victim," said my Lady, her lovely voice as unmoved as if she were speaking of some small domestic detail. There were times when I remembered that she was only half human; she could be as coldly indifferent to human life as any Olympian when the mood took her. Then with a more human note in her voice she said, "But it must not be Menelaus."

Wondering, as I often had, what my Lady's feelings really were for the husband she had left behind, I spoke up. "Better avoid any of the Kaphtui—the Cretans. Some of them will have been Dancers, and Kaphtui are quicker witted than their Argive allies. And avoid Odysseus: he's clever enough to find a way to defeat that net even if Athena didn't help him as she so often does...."

Penthesileia looked from one of us to the other, puzzled and perhaps a little dismayed. "But I don't know one Argive leader from another," she said. "How am I to know who I'm fighting?" I looked to my Lady: I was sure that the devious mind behind that lovely face had left no detail unthought of. Her smile told me that I was not wrong. "This is a strange war, Penthesileia," she said softly. "On ordinary days an Argive and a man of Ilium would kill each other on sight. But on some holy days a truce is declared, and at some of the shrines the people of Ilium and the Argives meet in peace, almost in friendship. There have even been cases of girls from the City taking Argive lovers on some of the feast days, The Mother and the Old Gods are worshipped here more than the Olympians and the Sacred Mating is still practiced to make the fields fertile. But even on ordinary feasts girls from the City go to titillate themselves by gazing at the mighty Argive warriors."

My Lady's eyes went from Penthesileia's face to mine and she smiled one of her "Olympian" smiles: she was enjoying this maneuvering of people as if they were pieces in a game. "At the next truce, M'pha," she said softly, "two girls from Ilium will go to look at the Argive warriors at the Temple of Thymbraean Apollo. And you will point out to Penthesileia the Argive leaders who are... available. And she will make her choice."

Chapter Three

THE TEMPLE

This was not the first trip I had made to the temple of Thymbraean Apollo on my Lady's business. There had been a time early in the war when she had almost persuaded Priam to return her to Menelaus and offer his own daughters in marriage to the chief leaders of the Greeks, cementing an alliance between the wealth of the City and the military power of the Argives. That scheme had been wrecked by pride and greed on both sides, chiefly the pride and greed of Agamemnon, the Argive commander-in-chief, and Hecuba who, as is common in kingdoms of the Old People, had as much power or more than her king-husband. In the Old Kingdoms the land and its fruits belong to the Queen, while the King besides being her overseer and baliff is responsible for war and trade.

I had carried some private messages for my Lady during those negotiations, and gained a great deal of respect for Odysseus, who had been the chief negotiater for the Argives. He was the cleverest man I had ever known, and the most ruthless, a good friend and a bad enemy. He and my Lady had a great deal of respect for each other, though little love was lost between them.

I was glad to see that Odysseus was not at the Temple on this occasion: I did not want his sharp eyes peering at Penthesileia, who despite the clothing of a woman of the City still looked too much the warrior-maiden. Most of the Argives in the temple hardly looked at us. If we had been flirtatious they would have responded eagerly, but so long as we behaved with decorum we would be ignored.

Most of the Argives who were at the Temple were

leaders of one of the thirty or so contingents of ships which made up the thousand-ship force that had followed Agamemnon to restore Helen to his brother, Menelaus, and to gain loot and glory for themselves. Year after year they had hung on stubbornly, refusing to admit defeat and return home. Not every man of them had been at the siege nine years: young warriors came from their homelands to replace the dead and wounded, just as fresh allies filtered into the City, lured by Priam's offers of wealth and future patronage.

The years had taken their toll, however, and most of them had little in the way of finery left: even on a peaceful occasion like this most of them wore their armor and wore or carried their helmets. Their swords were at their sides, but the long spears and the man-covering shields had been left in camp or at least in their chariots. It was easy enough to give their names and something of their histories to Penthesileia in a low voice as we strolled around the precincts of the Temple.

"All of these men are Argive 'leaders' in some sense," I told her, "and you'd fulfill the letter of Priam's requirement if you could kill or even wound one of them try seriously enough to put him out of action. But if you want to go back to the land of the Amazons covered with glory I suppose you'll have to kill someone, and probably one of the dozen or so really famous leaders. Someone like Ajax, son of Oeleus, the Locrian leader. He's not one of the great fighters but folk have heard of him. Rumor says he's a vicious man with few friends. Less chance with him of a comrade coming in to rescue him from your net."

Penthesileia gave a little shudder and said, "It seems so cold-blooded, choosing a man for slaughter as you'd pick a pig or a bullock. When someone comes at you in battle, kill or be killed, it's one thing, but this is... obscene." I liked her better for that speech but this was no time for her to start having qualms. "If you stand on the field of battle with weapons in your hands, any Argive here would do his best to kill you," I told her bluntly. "If you want to shut your eyes now, or go back to Ilium, do it, but if you meet one of them on the battlefield you may wish you'd watched for their weaknesses if you could. Take Ajax, for instance. Look how he squints. I'll wager his eyes are none too good. That's worth knowing, and you'd never have known it if you hadn't seen him with his helmet off."

I scanned the crowd, looking for someone else with a weakness I could point out and suddenly I felt as if a hand were squeezing at my heart. "Oh no!" I said before I could catch myself. Then I turned to Penthesileia and said with what dignity I could muster, "I must talk to a man I've seen here. He's a... fellow countryman. I'd better go alone but take a good look at him and please... if you see him in battle, pass him by."

Penthesileia was already half forgotten as I scurried across the temple precinct and put a hand on the arm of a young Kaphtui, unarmored and dressed only in a Kaphtui kilt and a cloak. He looked surprised for a moment, then grinned as he recognized me.

"Idomeneus, what are you doing here?" I hissed at him as I drew him into the shadow of a pillar.

He grinned at me and said, "Greetings to you, my ancient and revered aunt!" A few years separated us and we had always been good friends: this "ancient and revered aunt" thing was an old joke between us. His face grew more serious as he said, "We've had to increase our token force here, under Argive pressure. Father sent me as leader, partly because you were here. He judges that the Trojans can't last much longer and he wants you taken care of when the City falls."

I shook my head at him angrily. "I'll be all right; you know what I can do as a last resort. But you could be killed playing at being a warrior out on those fields of slaughter. And unless you have a sister I haven't heard of you're the heir to the throne of the Sea-Kings."

He shook his head. "No, there's no little Ariadne in the palace: I probably will be King of Crete. I say 'King' and 'Crete' deliberately; we're becoming more and more another Danaan kingdom. The days of M'nos the Sea King and Kaphtui the sea kingdom are fading, M'pha. But we're a strong and peaceful land, and the old palaces which were never rebuilt after the war are being replaced by villages. The mainlanders call us 'Crete of the Hundred Towns' and we're trying to keep the best of old ways and new."

I frowned. "Then why aren't you there in Kaphtu— Crete—helping your father and mother?"

He looked at me with serious eyes. "I'm doing just that," he said. "Helping protect the old and bring in the new. This combined expedition of all the Argive kindgoms and their Danaan allies is the biggest thing to happen in this age. By sending a few ships here we can establish ourselves as good Danaans: allies to be supported, not enemies to be raided. If we stayed neutral or allied ourselves with Troy... well, not everyone will get all the loot they want from Troy. If even a portion of this army stopped to raid Crete on the way home...."

I sighed, "Yes, I see. It sounds strange to hear you call Kaphtu Crete, as strange as hearing Ilium called Troy.

Danaan names, Danaan ways. I don't like it but I see the necessity. I've thought of myself as Kaphtui ever since I came to N'sos to leap the bull, but perhaps after this is over I'll go back to Karia. Lykia that is, now the kingdom's been divided. Curse it, Idomeneus, why can't things stay as they were?"

He shook his head and smiled a little sadly. "I know what you mean. Perhaps we've both heard too many stories about the great old days of legendary Sea-Kings and legendary Leapers. M'pha, why not go to Karia now, overland or on one of my ships. You've never seen a city sacked: it's a horrible confusion and you can't count on even the most powerful of our friends protecting you in the shambles."

I looked at him, half tempted, but then I remembered my promise. "I can't leave Helen," I said. "Not until she's back with Menelaus. I made a promise to... well, never mind. But this is as much my job just as what you are doing is yours. Perhaps we'll both survive, and if we don't...."

He looked at me with compassion. "I heard about your brother. I'm sorry, M'pha. Sarpedon and I were good friends. But remember...." He made a sign with his fingers, slowly unfolding the ringers of one hand and drawing the forefinger of the other hand across them near the palm. Of course we were both initiates of the Great Mystery at Eleusis.

"I know," I said. "We'll meet him again. But the parting is hard. He was the baby: Mother left him with me when she left Karia. I felt responsible, even when he was grown up. ..." Suddenly I remembered another responsibility. Looking back to where I had left Penthesileia I saw she was nowhere in sight. "Idomeneus!" I gasped. "Did you see the girl I was with?...Did you see where she went?"

"There was a girl looking at us when you first came over here, though I didn't see you together," he said. "She went off with one of the Argives, but I didn't get a good look at him. If it wasn't completely out of character I'd have sworn it was.... Wait, is that the girl? No, just another dark-haired Trojan. Who is your friend, she had a bit of the look of a leaper... not quite that, more like the Brauron girls."

"She's an Amazon," I said quietly, "and she'll be fighting for Troy. Please stay clear of her on the battlefield, Idomeneus." He nodded with a grave face. "I think I can, M'pha," he said. "Old friends or allies meet on the field sometimes and avoid each other, or even exchange gifts. You've probably heard how young Glaukos met Diomedes and they exchanged armor."

I smiled; it was one of the pleasanter tales of a sad war. "Yes, he was jeered at here because his armor was so much finer than that of Diomedes. But everyone knew, really, that he was lucky to escape with his life from a meeting with Diomedes."

Idomeneus nodded agreement. "He's a wild man and afraid of no one. He and Odysseus remind me of stories I've heard about my grandfather and Pirithous. Odysseus is the only man Diomedes respects just as Theseus was the only one Pirithous would listen to."

I looked at my young nephew, remembering that one of his two grandfathers had been Theseus the great warrior and adventurer and the other had been the last of the pure Kaphtui Sea-Kings. Perhaps he was not so out of place on this battlefield after all. But my unease about Penthesileia was increasing. "Where would my friend have gone with an Argive?" I said, my voice sharp with worry.

Idomeneus grinned. "Don't worry, Aunt dear," he

said. "If she's an Amazon he won't get very far with her. They're probably strolling in the garden of the temple. If we do the same we'll probably run into them."

My fears partly allayed, I strolled in the sweet-smelling gardens with Idomeneus, talking of our families and the days of our childhood. But it was hard to forget what was happening around us, with armored Argives walking the paths and jostling the worshipers from the City and the countryfolk who had come to the shrine for the feastday. The Argives gave way to Idomeneus respectfully, and it pleased me to see how much he was respected among them, young as he was.

One armored Argive, however, did not give way, but detained us with a respectful gesture. When he spoke I recognized the Spartan twang in his voice. "Excuse me. Prince Idomeneus, my Lady," said the Spartan. "I've been told that this lady is a companion of Queen Helen...."

Idomeneus looked at me to see if I wanted to talk to the man but I saw no harm in it. "I am one of the Queen's ladies," I told the Spartan, interested to see that after nine years of absence she was still "Queen Helen" to him.

"I'm Merionathes, Lady, of the King's Guards," said the Spartan. "The Queen may remember me...." Very likely she would: Helen's memory for people was remarkable. "I just wanted to say, my Lady," went on Merionathes, "that the soothsayers are promising us victory soon, and with Prince Hector dead perhaps they're right. When the city falls. Lady, we'd like to get to the Queen as soon as possible, to keep her safe...."

"Keep her safe," could have sinister connotations, but I felt that this man meant well. "The houses of the royal family are all near King Priam's House, just below the big white temple of Apollo you can see over the walls," I said quietly. "Queen Helen lives in the house called the House of the Golden Lintel: there are gilded figures carved above the door...."

The Spartan saluted and stepped back for us to pass but Idomeneus turned to him and said in a low voice, "This Lady is a kinswoman of mine. If you get to that house before I do...." The Spartan nodded and saluted again, and we walked on.

"Actually Danaan troops behave fairly well when a town is sacked," said Idomeneus. "In theory, the women are kept until the commanders take their pick. But there is always a bit of . . ."I nodded glumly. "A bit of freelance rape and murder," I said. "Especially after nine years of frustration, I know. But I'll have to take my chances, just as you will on the battlefield. At least I don't have to go out and fight by myself like Penthesileia. Idomeneus, I'm getting worried about her: surely we would have run into her if she were in the garden. ..."

Idomeneus looked around us. "Yes, I think so," he said. "The only other place is the meadow where some of the men do a little running or wrestling to pass the time..." I suddenly realized that Penthesileia might very well be tending to the business which had brought us to the Temple: an exercise ground would be an excellent place to observe the strengths and weaknesses of the Argive leaders. "I think she may be there." I told Idomeneus. "Can we go look?"

He led the way to a grassy meadow below the little hill on which the Temple stood: A few men were wrestling and others stood or sat or lay on the grass watching. At first I didn't see Penthesileia, and then two running figures caught my eye. One was Penthesileia, barefoot with her skirt kilted up, running as easily and swiftly as a deer. Beside her, easily keeping pace with her was a tall, long-limbed young Argive with broad shoulders and a face with jutting nose and thin lips which might look stern in repose, but which was now bright and smiling. As we watched the two reached a tree which must have been an agreed on goal post: both put on a burst of speed and they reached it together. They clung to the tree, laughing and gazing into each other's eyes each obviously delighted with the other.

"Is that your Amazon?" asked Idomeneus. "Yes," I said. "But the man...surely that can't be...."

Idomeneus nodded slowly, his face troubled. "Yes, it's the man you think it is; the slayer of Hector, the greatest of the Argive warriors—Achilles, the scourge of Troy!"

Chapter Four

IN BATTLE

I found that I couldn't tell Penthesileia who her running companion had been, even after we got back to the City. He had named himself to her simply as Fleetfoot, a common nickname for a good runner, and when I asked what they had talked of, Penthesileia blushed and shook her head. "Just nonsense," she said, "about what we would do if it weren't for...things. When we parted he said...no, it's too silly."

"What did he say, Penthesileia?" I asked, feeling a strange urgency.

"Just nonsense," she said, blushing again, "about how if I would come with him he'd forget the war and carry me off to his kingdom and make me his queen. Of course he didn't mean it."

"What if he did?" I said urgently. "He's a king—one of the Argive leaders. If he left the war and carried you off with him you would have eliminated one of the Argive leaders—you'd have fulfilled the obligation Priam put on you. Perhaps some god made Priam put it that way, to give you a chance... to give you both a chance."

The thought that she might save his life as well as her own appealed to her, I could see that and for a moment she hesitated. Then she shook her head. "It's all nonsense," she said. "I'm an Amazon, vowed to the Huntress. I have a kingdom to return to, if I can kill just one Argive leader. I won't stay after that, M'pha: I'll go home. Priam can't keep me...."

I opened my mouth to tell her of Cassandra's vision. Two paths, Cassandra had said: bright-faced in an

Argive's bed or dead on the battlefield. But how could I ask Penthesileia to trust Cassandra's prophecy when I didn't believe it myself...or did I?

I didn't give up: I did keep trying. But whatever dreams Penthesileia may have harbored in private, in public she was all business, training with her Amazons for her foray against the Argives. There was no question of her simply going out alone to find a victim: she would have to be protected from the Argive archers by her own Amazon archers, and have a screen of shields to duck behind if the arrows came too thick and fast.

Eventually after consulting with Diephobus and with her own Amazon officers, Penthesileia worked out a hollow square formation, with veteran City warriors in heavy armor on the outside, light-armed Amazons with bows on the inside and Penthesileia in the center. Any solid formation of City troops was a target for the Argive leaders and the formation would thus serve as a lure for a suitable victim as well as a protection for Penthesileia until she was ready to fight.

At the last moment I astounded myself by demanding to be part of the formation, carrying a net and trident like those Penthesileia was using. The Amazons, who were used to the idea of women fighting, had no objections, but at first Diephobus was adamantly opposed. There was only one way I could get around that, and I went straight to my Lady to plead my case. Surprisingly, she was willing to let me go.

"I've been talking to Cassandra," she told me, "or rather letting her talk to me. From her ramblings I've begun to think that this may not have been such a good idea. I'd feel a little better if you were with her to do what you could. Cassandra doesn't see you dying out there, for what that's worth. I have more confidence in my own feelings about you, M'pha. You're like me, a survivor. I wish I could say the same of Penthesileia." When Lady Helen told Diephobus to let me go, he agreed: I doubt if he had ever cared whether I lived or died, only whether my Lady might be displeased. So on a bright crisp morning not long after I found myself dressed in Amazon accouterments, standing with the rest of the formation just inside the Scaean Gate, a trident in one hand and a net in the other. I had two extra nets at my belt but I felt ridiculously exposed and unarmed.

I was trembling slightly and my palms were damp, but when the gate opened I was suddenly calm. I had been a Dancer: I had done the head-leap over the bull's horns. Now I was in a deadlier dance. But I had disciplined companions, men and women, beside me, and a job to do. Penthesileia's calm unhurried voice might have been that of the Mistress of the Dance on the bull court. "The lookouts report several chariots heading toward the fighting at the river," she said. "Only their leaders have chariots; those are the men we want. We'll help any of our troops we see and do what damage to the Argives we can, but our main task is to attract the attention of one of their chief men, and lure him in to fight."

At first those of us inside the square could see very little. A few arrows clattered on the shields of the City troops and the Amazons lifted their round horsemen's shields to turn any arrows that might be lofted over our outer ranks. Now we were in the thick of a skirmish between Argive common soldiers and some of the City troops, and the City soldiers in our square opened their ranks to let our archers step between them, fire their arrows and step back. We were doing so well that I was wondering why such formations were not used more, when I heard the sound of chariot wheels and the pounding of horse's hooves. "Get the horses, if you can," ordered Penthesileia, but the chariot paused only a moment, to let the full-armed warrior it carried alight, then clattered off, the chariot itself and the shield slung on the back of its driver protecting the horses.

The Argive warrior was not one of those I could recognize under his armor and helmet: I hoped that we had not caught some minor Argive noble rich enough to afford armor and a chariot. He came toward us at a shambling trot, uttering a loud cry which was intended to be terrifying. Our formation opened to let Penthesileia step out to face him, wearing only a leather jerkin sewn with metal pieces to turn arrows and a light helmet made of boar's tusks. The Argive stared at her, lifted his spear and then decided against throwing it. Brandishing the spear he strode toward Penthesileia, seemingly irresistible.

Her net snapped out and enmeshed him. With a roar and a crash he fell to the ground and in a moment her trident was at his throat. "Who are you, Argive?" she said with deadly sweetness. "Prodarces of Phylace," gasped the Argive. "Farewell, Prodarces," said Penthesileia and thrust with her trident. His body surged up for an instant, then slumped down in death. I turned my head for a moment and when I looked back Penthesileia's eyes were on mine.

"His brother was Protesilaus, a renowned warrior," I told her. He's dead and this man would have been king of Phylace." Penthesileia smiled bitterly.

"A hero's brother isn't enough, she said. "Give me the second net, M'pha: there was another chariot seen near here." With sinking heart I handed her a new net and fell into formation again. This man had been both stupid and slow: the kill had been deceptively easy. Was Penthesileia growing over-confident?

As we moved off again the soldiers of the City who had witnessed the combat gave a ragged cheer and joined our formation, making two ragged wings on either side of our square. The scattered Argive common soldiers took one look at our formidable looking group and began to retreat: some in good order, but others in outright flight. Penthesileia stopped our formation and let the archers fire after them.

One of the archers stopped suddenly with her bow half drawn, and knelt down to put her ear to the ground. She turned to Penthesileia and said laconically, "Horses, Lady. More than two, coming at a gallop." Penthesileia gave quick order and the formation closed up again, ready to withstand attack.

By now the sound of chariots being driven furiously could be heard by everyone and Penthesileia adjusted the formation a little to face the direction from which they were coming. Archers were ready, arrows on their bows, in case the horses came within range, but the Argive charioteers were wary, and dropped their heavily armed riders as soon as they came in sight of our formation.

The two heavily armored Argives did not attempt to rush us as Prodarces had: they came at a steady walk about a spear's length apart. Penthesileia could not possibly handle both of them and I realized with a sick feeling at the pit of my stomach that some premonition of something like this was the reason that I had insisted on coming with the Amazons. "You take the one on the left," I said to Penthesileia," in a voice as steady as I could manage, though I realized almost as soon as I spoke that I should have let her, the leader, tell me which one to take. But she merely nodded and moved close to the leading rank of heavily armed City warriors who screened our formation.

"Now," she said quietly and we stepped between the ranks to face our opponents. I had no time to look at what was happening with Penthesileia and her attacker, for my opponent threw his spear, almost as soon as I stepped clear of the ranks. It was a bad throw: I saw that it would miss me and walked toward my adversary without even looking at the spear. I heard a clang behind me as it hit the shield of a man in the front ranks.

I could hear the man cursing under his breath as he saw he had wasted his spear. His sword came out of the sheath with a rasp that set my teeth on edge and he began moving toward me again. Suddenly he stepped to one side for no apparent reason. My net was already in the air and I saw that it would miss him. I let go the cord immediately and reached for my belt where the extra net hung ready to my hand. The Argive, not quite realizing what I had thrown at him, lifted his shield to ward off whatever missile I had cast. The move obscured his vision for long enough to let me get my second net set: when he lowered his shield again I threw the second net and this time the net flew true, snapped open and settled over him. But he was close, too close. I could not just pull back and overbalance him. He would fall on me and could probably grapple with me through the net. I threw my trident at his face to keep him off balance and, grasping the cord of the net with both hands, ran to my right. He overbalanced and fell with a crash.

Immediately I knelt at his head, my dagger in my hand, seeking his throat. His eyes were wide and staring, his brow beaded with sweat. I could smell the rank tang of his fear. I knew that I could not press the knife home: the man was no threat to me and though I could kill in self-defense I could not slaughter a helpless man as Penthesileia had. A quick glance showed me that Penthesileia was still stalking her opponent, trying to set him up for the throw.

A hoarse whisper recalled my attention to my captive. "Lady, or goddess, whatever you are," the man said to me, "spare me. I am Machaon a son of Ascelepius, a Healer. Don't kill me. Lady."

I tried to make my face and voice as grim as possible as I said, "Why should I spare you to kill more Trojans?" I let the dagger prick his throat a little and felt him shudder. "Lady, Lady," came the urgent whisper. "Don't kill me and I will deliver Achilles, the great spearman into your hands. I have tended his wounds and know his weaknesses."

"Well?" I said, letting the contempt I felt for him show in my voice. But he was beyond any thought of shame and he babbled in the same rasping whisper. "Great Lady, listen, and have mercy. Everywhere on his body the flesh of Achilles is tough as leather: even if it is wounded it heals miraculously, and I think no weapon could harm him there. But his feet and ankles are tender and easily bruised: I have often treated him for scratches and bruises there, for he forgets that the flesh of his feet is not as invulnerable as that of the rest of his body. A spear or arrow in his foot would cripple him, put him out of action...."

"Enough, you have bought your life," I told Machaon, feeling as if I wanted to vomit.

"Scratch my cheek and ear, Lady," he begged. "It will bleed copiously and I will lie like a dead man until it is safe to crawl away." In my revulsion I slashed rather than scratched: if Machaon still lives he bears the scar of my knife. Then I rose from my knees, bloody dagger in hand, and looked to Penthesileia. She was in trouble: her net had not settled around her opponent's body but was caught over his head and shoulders. They were engaged in a deadly tug of war as she tried to keep him at a distance with her trident and pull him off balance, and he tried to close with her and get at her with his sword. His helmet had been knocked off and I could see an egg-shaped balding head and an ugly face distorted with fear and rage. Suddenly she thrust at his legs with her trident and pulled hard on her net: he overbalanced and sprawled on the ground unmoving: his unprotected head had come down on the rocky ground and he was stunned.

A cheer rose from the Amazons, but just then I heard the sound of two more chariots! With a groan I ran for my trident and for the first net I had thrown, frantically trying to refold it before the new Argive attackers were upon us. They came at a run, big men running with deadly swiftness. I was already crouched down trying to fold my net and I stayed there hoping to escape notice for a vital moment.

One of the new attackers, a veritable giant who could only be Big Ajax from Salamis, charged the armored City troops with a roar, ignoring Penthesileia. His companion ran straight for her, though, with a speed that made my heart sink. Surely only one man could run that fast in full armor! Penthesileia had her second net in her hand and her trident at the ready, but the figure before her seemed unstoppable as an avalanche. Yet, suddenly he did stop and stood staring at Penthesileia as she was now staring at him. In the sudden silence I could hear the chariots rattling away out of arrow range.

I saw again the stern, thin-lipped face I had seen in the Temple of Apollo; as I had feared, it was Achilles. But his voice was pleading as he spoke in a low tone that did not reach the ranks, but which I, crouched a spear's cast away, could hear. "My sweet runner," he said, "throw down your arms and become my captive and I will carry you to my black ship and sail home with you: forever after I will be captive to my captive who will become my wife and queen."

I could hear the agony in Penthesileia's voice as she said, "Fleetfoot, I am a daughter of Ares; I can't just tamely surrender. But if you lay down your arms too...." They stood looking at each other.

I will wonder to my dying day whether the great warrior could have bent his pride to yield to her request, and what she would have done if he had not. But suddenly the man she had brought down with her net rose up behind her: he must have been only pretending to be stunned. He hurled himself at Penthesileia's back and she lurched forward, her trident poking at Achilles's face as she reached out her hands to break her fall.

Achilles reacted with the deadly automatic response of the trained killer: his head moved to avoid the inadvertent thrust of her trident and the spear in his hand made a counterthrust. She had no shield to stop the thrust: her metal-inlaid leather shirt was worthless against the deadly sharpness of Achilles's spear. The bronze tip entered below her left breast and her heart's blood gushed out. With a little cry she crumpled to the ground, dead.

Chapter Five

THE SCAEAN GATE

Achilles dropped spear and shield with a mighty groan, and sank to his knees beside Penthesileia. He pulled his helmet from his head and cast it aside. Tears streaming from his eyes, he gently took her in his arms, murmuring incoherent endearments. I don't know how long I crouched there on the battlefield watching the scourge of Ilium weep over the fallen Amazon, but eventually the sounds of battle from where Ajax was doing grim destruction on Amazons and City troops seemed to reach his ears. Tenderly laying Penthesileia's body down, Achilles rose stiffly to his feet and bellowed,

"Ajax! Give over! Let them go!" When his call produced no apparent effect he took a few steps toward the battle and shouted again.

Before I realized what was happening the ugly bald Argive who had pushed Penthesileia onto Achilles's spear scuttled over to her body and raked at her eyes with clawed fingers. "Amazon bitch," he snarled. "Try to kill Thersites, will you!"

Achilles heard his voice and turned. When he saw what the man who had called himself Thersites had done, his face grew so terrible that I could scarcely bear to look at it. Thersites saw that look and began to babble. "I saved you, Achilles! The treacherous bitch would have got you to drop your weapons and then attacked you. You were always a fool for women, Achilles: look how you sulked over the captive girl Agamemnon took from you. Women are nothing but trouble. Look what Helen has caused...."

Achilles did not say a word, but raised his mighty

fist and struck Thersites one tremendous blow in the face. The man fell dead, his face shattered by the blow. "You should have died long ago," said Achilles in a voice drained of passion. "Odysseus should have killed you by the ships instead of beating you like the cur you are."

The gray eyes of Achilles suddenly saw me crouching and watching, but his killer instincts were stilled for the moment. He made a curiously tentative beckoning sign to me and I rose and walked over to face him. "What was her name?" he said in a strangely gentle voice.

"Penthesileia," I told him, "a princess of the Amazons."

Achilles bowed his head, his cheeks still wet with tears. "Peleus, my father, would have welcomed her," he said. "Our children would have rejoiced his old age. Now all the paths are closed but one." He looked at me searchingly. "Were you one of her companions?" he asked. When I nodded, not trusting myself to speak, he said, still in that gentle voice, "Help me to carry her back to Troy for honorable burial. I would bury her myself but some fool would laugh at me and I would kill them all."

"Achilles," said a deep voice from behind me, and I turned to see Big Ajax looming near us, his sword sheathed and his shield hung on his back. "I've called truce with the warrior girls," said Ajax, "those that are left. Will you let them have her body? They fought bravely and this one is as fair as a goddess, even in death."

"I will carry her myself," said Achilles. He knelt by Penthesileia's side and kissed her hands, then gently crossed them on her breast and took her body in his arms. "Let the Amazons make an honor guard for her," he told me. "Ask the Trojans to open the gate for us." Dropping my net and trident

I set off at a run for the City. What the guards would make of an unarmed Achilles surrounded by Amazons and carrying the dead princess I did not know, but I wanted nothing to mar Penthesileia's last return to Ilium. If only I could reach King Priam, who owed Achilles a debt of honor for the return of Hector's body. . . .

When I reached the Scaean Gate it was opened wide enough to let me slip in: as always there were curious folk waiting there to get news of the battles. Some of these were fighting men put out of action by wounds and others were older men of importance. I had hoped that the King might be among them today, since he had seemed to have such hopes of Penthesileia's help against the enemies of the City. But the guard captain at the Gate dashed my hopes. "King Priam is in Apollo's temple. Lady, beseeching the Bright Lord on behalf of the City and its defenders," he said. "Prince Paris is on the walls not far from here, if you want one of the King's family."

I hesitated, but Paris was better than no one. If I tried seeking Priam in the temple I might be too late. Paris at least knew me and had some respect, if little liking, for me. Paris was capricious: if I caught him in a good mood he might help me.

I found him easily enough standing on the walkway atop the walls. He was in light armor with his bow in his hand. He had been abandoned in the wilds as a child because of one of those mischief-making prophecies that seem to be so often made at the birth of royal children, and which so often lead to ruin when an attempt is made to evade them. Paris had been brought up by a shepherd family and had only been discovered to be the lost prince when he was already a young man. Thus he had missed a good deal of the usual training of a young noble and was still a good deal better with peasant weapons like bow and sling than he was at fighting like a nobleman with spear and sword in heavy armor. I suspected Hecuba's scheming behind the convenient shepherd who had "found" him and behind his dramatic "discovery" as the prince. Still he knew that his parents had cast him out when he was a baby, and perhaps that accounted for a good deal in his character: the way he used his easy charm to captivate others, but fled from any deep relationships.

That charm was to the fore today as he greeted me with elaborate courtesy and with praise for my courage in taking part in the battle. When I told him of Penthesileia's death his face darkened. "Poor girl," he said, "and poor Ilium too. One more defender dead, one ally the less, one more hope dashed. And by Achilles again, curse him! He strides about invulnerable as a stone tower, and slaughters us as he wills!"

One could never tell how genuine an emotion was with Paris, but he always seemed genuinely moved if you were: he echoed your emotion and somehow increased it. I felt a little spurt of rage at Achilles and blurted out, "Not so invulnerable. Prince Paris. A man on the battlefield who was at my mercy babbled Achilles's weakness to save his own life. It seems the 'tower' has weak foundations; his feet and ankles are softer and more easily injured than the rest of his body."

Paris was motionless for a moment, his eyes glittering but his face revealing nothing. Somehow his silence made me uncomfortable and I rushed into speech: "Lord Paris, Achilles is bearing Penthesileia's body here for burial. Can you . . . will you see that a truce is kept while he brings the body to the gate? He means to do her honor, it's no trick of the Argives. Surely the City owes her a seemly burial, rather than having her body fought over as dogs fight over a scrap of meat."

Paris looked at me a long moment, his eyes inscrutable, but when he spoke his words seemed all I could have hoped for. "I will give the order for battle to cease. Run to Athena's temple and ask the priestesses to come to receive her body: when the Argives see the priestesses at the gate they will be sure that we mean no attack on them."

It seemed gracious and fitting that the body of the warrior princess and priestess of the Huntress should be received by the hands of women dedicated to Athena, Maiden and Warrior. Stammering a few words of thanks to Paris I ran off on my errand. By the time I returned with the priestesses the gate was open and there were no armed men in evidence, though I was sure that they were within call in case of Argive treachery. Achilles and the Amazons were already in sight, walking slowly toward the City. When they saw the white-robed women at the open gate they came toward it, still at the same slow pace. Achilles had his helmet on and his sword at his side: it would be a bold foe who attacked the great warrior in his sorrow, and if a sizable band of City warriors came out at him, Achilles's famous running ability would probably take him out of danger. Still it was a measure both of his courage and of his desire to honor Penthesileia that he came almost to the gate before he waited for the priestesses to meet him and take her body.

I stood at the gate awkwardly, feeling out of place in the solemn band of priestesses. Achilles, his face stony but his eyes bright with tears, handed Penthesileia's body tenderly into their hands. His voice was hoarse and strained as he said to the chief priestess, "Bury her with honor. Your city holds nothing more precious than her body" he said.

Then he turned, abruptly and started walking slowly away from the gate. The gates were closed by men who had been standing behind them almost before the priestesses and the Amazon honor guard were inside the City. It was not the haste of men who feared to see their greatest enemy at the open gate of their City: their movements were disciplined, swift and almost stealthy. Suddenly a suspicion came into my mind and I looked around for Paris. These men had been given orders:

orders I had not heard since Paris had conveniently sent me away to the temple. What else had Paris ordered?

Suddenly, Paris himself appeared at the door of one of the guard houses beside the gate. Beside him was a young man who had the look of one of Priam's sons: since Priam boasted of fifty sons I could never keep them all straight. Paris and the young man stepped to the gate and one of the soldiers who had closed it slid back a wicket which was built into the gate to let the guards inspect those seeking entrance.

I was so close that through the wicket I could see Achilles walking slowly away. His back was protected by the shield slung over it, but below his kilt of metal-studded leather strips his legs were bare: his greaves protected his shins but not the calves of his legs or his heels. Paris had his bow in one hand and a wicked-looking black arrow in the other.

I stepped forward, ready to protest, even to cry out to warn Achilles, but the young man beside Paris turned and looked at me. The eyes that met mine were not human eyes: this was not the son of Priam or of any earthly king. The face still seemed the face of a young man of Ilium, but the timbre of his voice revealed the Olympian behind that illusion as he said, "Peace, M'pha. The time has come to make an end. As well this way as another."

He turned back, assuming my obedience, but even if I had dared to defy an Olympian it would have been no use. Paris loosed his arrow and the illusion wavered for a moment as the Olympian concentrated his powers on the arrow. It did not need the golden bow slung across his back to tell me that a greater Archer than Paris was here. Paris gave a little "hah" of triumph as he peered out after his arrow, then stepped back and gestured for the gates to be opened. Did he think to win glory for himself by fighting a crippled Achilles? Even with one foot wounded Achilles would be more than a match for Paris....

But when the gates swung open Achilles was already in his death throes. The black arrow which protruded from his heel must have been fearfully poisoned. Paris sometimes boasted of the herb lore he had learned from his first wife, a Wild Girl from the mountains.... Even as I watched, Achilles gave a last convulsive shudder and went limp, killed by Paris and Apollo at the Scaean Gate.

Chapter Six

OENONE

Paris strode forward followed by armed men from the guard house. He cried out, "The tower of the Argives is fallen. His armor is mine; his body I will treat as he treated that of Hector, my brother...." But suddenly there was a booming cry and Ajax appeared from the shelter of a little hillock where he had hidden himself. No doubt he had feared some attack on Achilles, but he had not anticipated its swiftness or deadliness. For a moment Paris wavered, but then I could see him brace himself. "He's alone," he told the City troops who had followed him out the gate to retrieve the body of Achilles. "Surround him and keep him off balance," he ordered them. "Don't let him get any of you into an individual fight, harry him until I can get a shot in."

And harry Ajax they did, like a pack of dogs around a lion. When he tried to charge at them they gave way and when he got far enough from the body of Achilles some of them started to drag it off toward the City. Ajax rushed back, scattering them as a hawk scatters doves but after that he was pinned down, not daring to get too far from the body lest they drag it so near the City that rocks or hot oil could be hurled at him from the walls. Archers on the City walls were already aiming shafts at him, and he had to keep his shield up lest some marksman take aim on his face and send a lucky arrow into his face or throat.

Paris stood back a little from the skirmish, an arrow on his bowstring, waiting for an opening. Dressed in light armor as he was he could not have been expected to engage Ajax hand to hand, but in any case Paris was no match for the giant Ajax, who was one of the best Argive warriors, perhaps the best now that Achilles was dead. Ajax had positioned himself astride the body of Achilles, and was using his massive spear to keep the City warriors at bay, holding it near the butt and swinging it in a deadly circle that kept his attackers at a distance.

When Ajax saw Paris hovering in the background he let out an agonized roar, "Come fight like a man, you mincing coward!" he bellowed. "You shot a better man in the back when he came in peace to honor one of your allies. The Amazon girl was a better man than you'll ever be." Shifting his grip on his spear with marvelous dexterity the giant Argive flung his spear at Paris with deadly speed and force. But though it must be hard to dodge a flung spear when you are encumbered with heavy armor and a man-covering shield, it is not all that difficult when you are lightly armored as Paris was. As I had done with Phyrgos, Paris watched for the tensing of his opponent's muscles, waited for the point in the throw when the spear was almost launched and its direction could not be changed and then stepped aside. The spear missed Paris and flew well past him before it clattered down onto the stony ground.

Paris loosed an arrow that splintered on the helmet of Ajax: a few fingers lower and it would have ended the fight. "I have plenty of arrows," he jeered, "but you've thrown away your only missile, Ajax. Chase me round the walls if you like, you lumbering bully, as Achilles did my brother. But when you return you'll find that the body of Achilles and his splendid armor are safely inside the unconquerable walls of Ilium. You're not the runner Achilles was, Ajax: I'll lead you a merry chase!"

Ajax had not yet drawn his sword and this made the City warriors bold enough to press their attacks on him with their spears. Twice he tried, with his incredible quickness of hand to snatch the spear from one of his attackers but the bronze spearpoints were too long and too sharp: even with his great reach he could not grab the spears by their wooden shafts, nor could he have held them by the points without cutting his hand to the bone.

With a snarl, Ajax stooped down. I half expected him to sling the body of Achilles over his shoulder and start fighting his way back to the Argive lines. But suddenly he was on his feet again. He had slipped his left arm out of the shield handles and shrugged the shield back so it hung by its strap from his back. He grasped in both hands a jagged rock so big it seemed incredible that he could lift it: he raised it over his head with a roar and the City warriors fell back: if that rock hit a shield or helmet with the force Ajax could put behind it the man it hit would be lucky to escape with only broken bones.

But with a tremendous effort Ajax hurled the rock at Paris. When Paris had evaded the spear he had moved to the right; seeing the rock coming at him he jumped right again, but Ajax must have allowed for that too-predictable move, for Paris's leap took him straight into the path of the flung boulder: he fell to the ground with his chest smashed.

Ajax let out a booming laugh and stooped again. The City warriors shrank back, but this time Ajax did pick up Achilles, shield and all, and hold him to his chest with one massive arm. Achilles's body and shield defended Ajax in front, and his own slung shield protected his back. An ordinary man could not have walked with that weight, but Ajax strode ahead like a human battering ram, knocking the City warriors out of his way. With no one to rally the attack the City warriors fell back to the gate, which had remained open all this time.

A groan from Paris galvanized me: I ran out the gate, shrieking at the warriors not to leave their leader on the field. Shamefacedly they turned back, but I reached Paris first, dropping to my knees beside him and trying to assess how badly he was hurt.

There was blood coming out of his mouth and more came out as a rattling cough racked his tortured body. He made a feeble gesture and I put my head close to his. "Make them... carry me... to Mount Ida..." came his strained whisper. "My first wife... the nymph Oenone... lives on the slopes... my men know... where."

Marveling at this return of the dying man to the wife he had abandoned to woo and carry off Helen, I passed on the message of Paris to the warriors who had come up to take him to the City. One of them nodded, "I know the place, yes," he said. "The less he's moved the better: we'll make a litter of spears and carry him there. It should be safe enough: the Argives will call truce to mourn Achilles. Would you come with us, Lady? We could use your help to ease him on the way and when we reach the Grove we'll have to send a woman in: it's death for a man to go in uninvited."

That journey is another thing that often comes back to me in dreams. We trudged steadily up the long slope which led to the heights of Mount Ida. The ground grew more and more rocky and rough but the path was fairly well worn and those who carried Paris were able to keep him fairly steady. Still some jolts and bumps were inevitable, and the groans of Paris grew more and more feeble and his breathing rougher and harsher. I tried to shade his face from the sun and when we crossed a little stream I washed his face as gently as I could. One of the soldiers took off his helmet and filled it with water and I carried it cradled in my arm; and occasionally sponged Paris's brow with a rag torn from my undertunic and wrung out in the water.

When we reached the Grove I knew we had arrived at our destination. The trees were well-grown despite the rocky wilderness around them and the grass under the trees was green and lush, but not a man in the party dared to rest on the grass or even seek the shade of the trees. It was not a human place and the shade of those trees was not inviting, despite the glare of the sun on the barren rocks around us. The Grove held its secret and its mystery, though it stood in plain sight in the light of day.

I sighed and laid aside what few accouterments of war I still had by me: my boar's-tooth helmet and the heavy dagger I had carried into battle as a last resort. Then I walked as steadily as I could into the woods. When I came to a little glade I sat on a mossy stone by a small stream and waited. Presently I felt a prickling on the back of my neck which told me that I was not alone. I said as quietly and calmly as I could, "If you are Oenone, I have a message for you."

"Go away," said a voice behind me, and the woods seemed to echo the words, "Go away," "Go away." I let the wave of panic fear that accompanied those words wash over me and recede: trying to fight it would make it worse. I looked up at the sky above the trees and said in a voice I tried to keep from trembling, "Pan also is a child of Zeus. I claim the strangers' welcome."

When I looked down the Wild Girl was standing before me, naked except for a wreath of flowers on her head and another about her loins. The green eyes looked at me unblinkingly and a little half smile played around her lips. "You're very strong," she said. "Perhaps I'll listen to what you want to tell me." I had caught her attention for the moment, but her attention might easily be distracted by a bird, an animal, even the wind in trees. If she ran off I would have to wait for her to return: searching for the Wild People only raised their half-mischievous, half-timid instinct for evasion.

"Paris is outside the Grove, dying," I told her. "He wants you." Her eyes were blank for a moment. "Paris?" she said. "Oh, you mean Alexander. They called him Paris when he went to the Mountain of Houses. He said he'd come back to me, but he didn't. He went off across the salt-water and carried home the golden girl. And he never came here again. She came once though, this golden girl. We couldn't frighten her either."

It was news to me that Lady Helen had visited the Grove, but I was not too surprised. It was very like her to want to meet the former wife of Paris. I wondered what the two women had found to talk of, but time was running out for Paris. "Will you see Alexander?" I persisted. "He's at the edge of the Grove. He was wounded outside the City—the Mountain of Houses as you call it—and carried here. He may not last much longer."

"Oh, I don't mind seeing him," she said casually. "Wait here, I'll get him." She strode off and vanished into the wood. I hoped that the men with Paris had the sense to hide their eyes as soon as they caught sight of her. Men who gazed too long on the Wild Girls often lost their wits: it was called being "nymph-struck."

Oenone was back in a moment, carrying Paris easily in her arms. She laid him on the ground beside the stream and squatted on her heels beside him looking at him curiously. "He's still very beautiful," she said, "or would be if he weren't damaged." Her voice aroused Paris and he opened his eyes and looked at her and said her name.

"Oenone," he said, "You can cure me... Helenus told me I'd be wounded... and to come to you. He said if you'd cure me I'd live a long life...." The voice of Paris was a little stronger, there was even a little of his old cajoling charm in it as he said, "Please, Oenone...we were happy together once...."

The Wild Girl looked at him thoughtfully. Just when you thought the Wild Folks were more animal than human they often surprised you, and she surprised me now. "Will you leave the golden girl and come back to me, Alexander?" she asked.

"Oh yes, my love!" said Paris eagerly, raising himself a little and then sinking back with a wince.

She shook her head. "So long as the Mountain of Houses is there I don't trust you," she said. "Perhaps I'll help the Northern Men bring it down. Will you tell me how to do that, Alexander?"

He bit his lip, then answered with a show of reluctance but without hesitation. "There's a small wooden statue of Pallas in the Temple of Athena. The Olympians swore that so long as we kept it safe the citadel would never fall. By now that may be the only thing preserving the City...."

The Wild Girl smiled a wicked little smile and said, "This girl and the men who brought you... we don't like mortals near the Grove. Shall we send the Fear on them and hunt them down?"

This time Paris didn't even pretend reluctance. He managed a sort of shrug, though he winced again at the movement. "Take them if you like," he said, "then no one will know I'm here...."

The nymph's green eyes met mine for a long moment while my breath and heart seemed to stop. Then she smiled at me and said, "Take him away. I don't want him."

She started to walk away and I felt that I owed it to myself if not to Paris to say something. "He'll die if we take him away, Oenone," I said.

She looked down at Paris for a long moment and said in a musing tone, "The shepherds called him Alexander: it means 'Defender' in their tongue," she said. "He protected the flocks from wolves and the folk from bandits. He even stood up to us when we hunted some of the shepherds who came too close to the Grove looking for lost sheep. That's how I met him first. Now he'd leave the woman he carried off, help bring down his home, betray you and the others who carried him here to me. And all this so that he may live to grow old. No, child, you can take this man away. My Alexander is dead already: I think he died long ago."

Chapter Seven
APHRODITE'S REVENGE

Mercifully, Paris lost consciousness when he heard Oenone's words: it made it easier for me to get him to the edge of the woods. Despite their weariness the men were eager to get away from the Grove: they picked up the litter again and bore him toward the City as quickly as they could without jolting him too badly. The grizzled warrior who had guided us to the Grove waited until we were well away from the Grove and then asked me what had happened. I told him only that Paris had asked Oenone for healing and she had refused. He sighed. "Pity a few more folk didn't say 'no' to him earlier," the old warrior said sadly. "The shepherd folk spoiled him because they could see he was noble-born, and once the Queen got him back she wouldn't let King Priam refuse him anything. Even your Lady didn't say him nay, and see what's come of that. When he was born, the Queen dreamed that she'd been delivered of a fiery torch that burned the City down: that's why the King ordered him abandoned in the wilds."

The man sighed and went on, "Well, the prophecy is coming true, right enough, but if they hadn't cast him out the City might have burned in a nobler cause. Some say the King shouldn't have taken him back into the City when he came to the Festival and dazzled everyone with his skill and charm, but once the Queen saw him and found he was the child she'd lost I don't think the King could have kept him out If he'd tried. Prince Paris would have had his supporters: perhaps the army before the City would have been Paris's and some group of allies pledged to put him on the throne. Perhaps even Argive allies. Your Lady needn't blame herself: the

Argives were bound to try to loot the City sooner or later."

I repeated all of this to Lady Helen when I told her all that had happened since I left the City that morning. Paris had died on the way back: his body rested now in the hall of the House of the Golden Lintel. My lady had observed all the ceremonies of mourning but now alone with me in her private rooms she made no pretense of sorrow. "Yes, your old soldier was right," she said. "Agamemnon and others used to count over the 'gold of Troy' in their councils and debate how they could unite the Argives and their allies to loot that gold. I've always known that I was a pretext. And it wasn't Paris I didn't say 'no' to but his Olympian patroness who handed me over to him as one ruler gifts another with a pretty slave girl."

She looked out over the city from her window with a brooding look. "That doesn't mean that I'm without guilt," she said. "I told myself that I'd do my husband and daughter no good by letting Aphrodite blast me in her rage, but even that may have been self-deception. I'd have left them a memory to be proud of at least. And I don't believe Zeus would have let Aphrodite kill me. The worst she could have done would have been to steal my beauty, but I couldn't face that. Menelaus worshiped me, but I didn't dare find out if it was me or my beauty he worshiped."

I was embarrassed by the emotion in her voice and said with an attempt at flippancy, "Most men would claim that they'd honor a woman who chose faithfulness at the price of beauty. But I wonder how many really would...."

My Lady gave a little smile and said, "The only man I know of who chose his wife for her character rather than her looks is Odysseus. It's one reason I respect him as well as fear him for his ruthlessness and cunning. His wiles will do more to bring the City down than all Achilles's strength could. But the people in the streets are rejoicing because Achilles is dead: they think his death may make the Argives abandon the siege. There's something false in the honor they're paying Paris for killing Achilles; in their hearts many of them are probably glad enough to trade the lives of Penthesileia and Paris for the life of Achilles. Poor Amazon... Poor Paris too. The nymph was right in a way, something in Paris died long ago. Perhaps the last blow for him was Hector's death. Hector never blamed Paris for the war, or me either. Andromache does though, blame me I mean, and so do many of the women who've lost their men. Perhaps they're sick enough of me and the war to influence their men to give me back and make peace."

There was little hope of that, we both knew. Just as Lady Helen had only been an excuse for the war beginning, she was only an excuse for the war continuing. The City wanted to end Argive raids forever, not encourage future expeditions by returning Helen, along with the indemnities the Argives would no doubt demand. But the pretense had to be kept up that the war was for Lady Helen, and my Lady's eyes flashed when some of her friends in the inner councils let her have word that the talk was of giving her to another of Priam's sons as a gesture of defiance to the Argives. "I won't stand for it!" she stormed.

"You don't have to, Helen," said a voice from behinds us and we turned to see standing there in all her Olympian glory, Aphrodite, the cause of my Lady's troubles if not of the City's.

My first impulse was gratitude, but Helen's face was wary: she knew Aphrodite better than I did. "What do you mean, Bright Lady?" she asked in a voice which mingled skepticism with enough respect to avoid calling down the Olympian's wrath.

Aphrodite shrugged her lovely shoulders; dangerous as she was it was a delight merely to look at her. Even my Lady's beauty was lessened beside that of the goddess, though still glorious. It was not like the moon and the sun together, but like the sun and a mirror reflecting it with a lesser but still blinding light.

"Paris was only an incident," said Aphrodite with a smile and a lift of one delicately arched eyebrow that gave her face a look of delighted mischief. "Now the real plan begins. Zeus has promised that Aeneus, my son by Anchises, will become the founder of a great nation after Ilium falls. You will be his queen and consort and your beauty and wisdom will become a golden legend."

Helen lifted a hand in protest but the Olympian swept on. "Do you know what else he promised?" she said with an enthusiasm that was hard to resist. "I've known for a long time that you could live in the land of the Olympians. You can be as immortal as we are if you choose, Helen. And Zeus has promised me that if the man you choose to share the rest of your life with has enough Olympian blood he too will become an immortal. You and Aeneus, together forever...."

"No, Aphrodite," said Lady Helen, and I could have told the Olympian that when my Lady spoke in that tone of voice she could no more be moved than the mighty mass of Mount Ida itself. The goddess was so taken aback at this determined opposition that for a moment she was speechless and my Lady went on in the same quiet voice. "I let you force me to go with Paris, I let you push me back into his bed after Menelaus defeated him in a fair fight and you saved him from death and stirred up the war again by using Pandarus to break the truce. But this time you won't do it. Aeneus is a good man but I don't want him and he doesn't want me and he won't even with the bribe of immortality thrown in. I'm not your plaything. Aphrodite, to be given first to your favorite, then to your son."

"And what do you want, girl?" said the goddess with ominous sweetness.

Helen shrugged and her face was weary. "Not a man who only wants me because I'm the most beautiful woman in the world, or because he'll cheat death by marrying me. I'm tired of all that. I don't know if I still want Menelaus or if he still wants me, after ten years. But I want my daughter, Hermione, and I want my home. So if Menelaus will take me back I'll go with him. This City will fall eventually; you've let that slip. I'm tired of being a legend: I'll go home and be a wife and mother for a while."

I think that even Aphrodite realized that threats would be of no use, but there was an icy glitter in her eyes that boded ill for my mistress. "You'll frustrate my plans, will you, girl?" she said. "Well, I see that I can't make you, and there's a limit to what your Father will let me do to you. You still have his promise, for whatever that's worth to you. But what is in my charge I can give or take and even Zeus won't stop me. Pick up your mirror, girl, and look. Do you like what you see?"

When I turned my eyes from Aphrodite to my Lady my involuntary gasp must have told her what to expect, but, with a steady hand, she reached for her mirror, which had been a wedding gift from my mother. When she had looked long into it she turned to Aphrodite with dignity: I had never admired or loved her more. "It's quite a good face," she said. "It reminds me of my mother's when I last saw her. If what was beyond this was your gift it was a gift which has caused me more sorrow than joy. I can live with this."

"You'll have to," sneered the Olympian, but I knew she was defeated and she knew it too. She vanished in a cloud of golden sparks and Lady Helen and I were alone.

After the first shock I found that I liked Helen's new face: it looked both sensible and kind. "It's more like you, somehow," I blurted out. "More like you are inside." She smiled and raised her hands to her face, touching her cheeks almost caressingly. It was a graceful gesture and I suddenly realized that there was much that Aphrodite had not been able to take away: the grace of my Lady's every movement, the proud stance of a woman who had always been admired and catered to.

"It's not quite such a shock as Aphrodite planned," Helen said wryly. "Your mother taught me once to make up my face to look like an old woman: it's a trick I've used once or twice when it was too dangerous to look like myself. And with the life I've led I might well have looked like this now if Aphrodite hadn't used her Olympian powers to keep me young. Perhaps what she took from me was really hers after all: an enchantment, something out of nature."

I shook my head. "You're a daughter of Zeus," I said. "You have every right to stay young while mortal beauty fades...."

She shrugged and was about to speak when the door opened and Aethra entered. She concealed her first shock better than I had, but she had always been a secretive, self-contained woman who gave away very little of what she felt. She picked up a garment which had slipped to the floor and said quietly, "I see that you and Aphrodite have come to a parting of the ways, Lady Helen. Well, most women must face the loss of youth's beauty sooner or later. My son always said that your beauty was the least important thing about you, though everyone else thought it was the most important thing."

She could hardly have said anything that would have pleased or consoled Helen more: to be reminded of the man who had loved her for herself and not for her face was just what she needed now. Her head lifted and a smile gave her face for an instant a shadow of its old beauty. "They were talking of giving me to Deiphobus," she said with what seemed to be genuine amusement. "He's in for a shock."

Priam and his Council did indeed give my Lady to Deiphobus without more than a purely formal gesture of asking consent. The way that Deiphobus's eagerness turned to dismay when he saw the change in Helen was a matter for either laughter or tears, but it was easy enough to laugh. The admiration of Deiphobus for my Lady had never gone beyond her face: he was no Theseus to love her for her wit and spirit. The marriage was only a form: he was almost indecently eager to accept her excuses of mourning for Paris and postpone the wedding night. My Lady, Aethra and I continued to live peacefully in the house of the Golden Lintel. In fact, life was more peaceful without Paris's moods and tantrums.

We were not quite prisoners in the house, but once Priam learned what had happened he let it be known that he felt that strict seclusion was appropriate to our "house of mourning." He clung to his pretext for war as stubbornly as if he would rather bring down Ilium than admit that the prize his army fought for had become, by the standards of men like Deiphobus, worthless.

My Lady smiled bitterly when she told me of Priam's

hints. "I suspect that I could walk out of the City during this truce," she said, "and no one would know me or stop me. But the Argives would be as little likely to want me back now as Priam is to send me back. I was always a pretext for this war and that's my only value to them now. This has to end, M'pha. I've sent some messages by means I didn't want to involve you in, just in case they were discovered. But I do want you to loiter near the gate the next few days. When you see someone you recognize, and you will, bring him to me."

I almost didn't recognize the result of Helen's messages though, when it came. My attention was caught as I loitered at a market stall near the Scaean Gate by boisterous laughter from the guards, and I strolled over to see what they were laughing at. It was a beggar, an Argive by the look of him, covered with filth and sores and with a leg twisted at an odd angle. He stood propped on a crutch pouring out words in a sort of ingratiating whine.

"Oh, I was a great man among the Argives, a great man, came in my own ship with many fine fellows. But you terrible Trojans killed my men and crippled me, then I fell afoul of the terrible Agamemnon, got on his bad side,and he had me scourged out of the camp." His back showed the scars of a whipping all right but from his filth and sores if he had ever been a "great man" among the Argives it must have been long ago. He had the look of a longtime camp-follower and a scrounger; there were plenty of them around the City as well as around the Argive camp. They all claimed to be warriors crippled in battle but few of them really were. Soldiers are superstitious and think it lucky to toss a morsel to a beggar, so every ne'er-do-well in the Troad scrounged at the Argive camp or around the soldiers' quarters in the City.

The beggar was going on now about the girls he'd bedded in his prime and making the guards laugh, with his bawdy wit. I almost turned away, but suddenly a characteristic turn of the head caught my eye and suddenly I saw beyond the rags and filth to the powerful torso and arms, the legs a little too short for the body, the great domed head and shaggy brows. There, standing inside the Scaean gate jesting with the guards, was one of the most formidable enemies of Ilium, as clever as he was ruthless: the Great Schemer, Odysseus, King of Ithaka!

Chapter Eight

THE HORSE

I took a deep breath and stepped up to the captain of the guards. He saluted me and silenced the whining voice of Odysseus with a casually brutal blow to his mouth. "Peace, scarecrow," he said. "How can I serve you. Lady?" I saw the deepset eyes of Odysseus flash for a moment and I would not have liked to be that guard captain if he ever came near Odysseus on the field of battle.

"I serve Lady Helen," I told the guard captain. "It's a custom in her country for a widow to give some cast-off garments of a dead husband to the poorest beggar she can find: it keeps further evil from the house. This is certainly the poorest beggar I've seem...." The guard captain laughed obsequiously and pushed Odysseus toward me.

"He's all yours. Lady, but keep upwind of him," said the guard, then sharply to Odysseus, "Here you: follow this Lady and if she has any complaint to make at you I'll cut out your guts and make you eat them." Odysseus whined and groveled, and when I turned to go followed me at a respectful distance.

When we reached the house I left Odysseus in the hall under the disapproving eye of our steward; and went in search of Helen. She seized on my idea of some Spartan superstition about beggars and elaborated it. "Take this man to the courtyard and sluice him off a bit," she ordered. "Then bring me a basin of water: the ceremony requires that I wash his feet. Keep all of the servants away while I do it; I don't want them gaping."

The steward saluted respectfully and returned presently with a damp and shivering Odysseus, bedraggled but at least no longer offensive to the nose. Then he brought a basin of water and stalked off, a picture of offended dignity.

Lady Helen knelt and began washing the feet of Odysseus: she was as unlikely to neglect any detail of her charade as Odysseus was to neglect any detail of his disguise. The keen gray eyes of Odysseus searched Helen's face, but he made no comment, waiting for her to speak. "I wanted you to see me, Odysseus," she said quietly. "It's something you'll need to take into account. I'm willing to help you now, in the way I refused to help before, but I have some conditions."

Odysseus nodded gravely and said in his deep, persuasive voice, "We're not likely to quarrel over that. Queen Helen. I've always thought that Troy would fall when you decided to help us. It's taken longer than I thought, but the end is in sight now. I may see Penelope now before she has gray hair and Telemachus before he has sons of his own."

"I want it over as much as you do," said my Lady. "But I know what happens when a city is sacked. Can there be some kind of apparent withdrawal of the Argive forces? If there is, a good many people will leave the City for visits to the country just because they've been cooped up so long, and I can use my influence in various ways to get others to go. There will still be plenty of loot and plenty of unfortunates for you to take captive, but it will make things a good deal better if many folk are out of the City. The children especially: I worry about them."

Odysseus nodded. "I can persuade Agamenmon to make an apparent withdrawal, yes. In fact, it will be a good way to take Troy unaware. I have a scheme to get a small contingent inside the city to open the gates when we return:

I won't involve you. But I do need your help on something. There's an Olympian promise that the city won't fall so long as some treasure is preserved here. We wrung that much from Prince Helenus when we captured him, but he wouldn't tell us what it is."

"If Helenus knew, so will his sister Cassandra," said my Lady. "She trusts me, and I think I can get it out of her...." Suddenly I remembered the Grove and the harsh voice of a dying man.

"Paris knew!" I cried. "When he was dying he said... there's a small wooden status of Pallas in the Temple of Athena: so long as it's safe Troy can't fall...." Suddenly my voice died as I realized that my words meant the end of the City.

Aethra, who had been standing silent in the background, spoke now. "I know Athena's priestess," she said, "and I know where something very special, something she won't show even to me is kept. There's a chest built into the base of the image of Athena...."

Odysseus nodded. "That tells me enough. Lady Aethra," he said. "If the priestess reckons on the power of the Gray-eyed Lady to keep anyone from touching that chest, as no doubt she does, then she forgets that the Daughter of Zeus has her favorites." He did not need to say that he was the chief of these favorites, with his friend Diomedes not far behind him. As if in answer to my thought Odysseus went on, "Diomedes and I will be back during the night of the dark of the moon. I'd take my chances on snatching it now but I'll never get out the gate without being searched for whatever gifts Lady Helen gave me. The guards are already licking their lips over what they believe they'll get out of me: better give me a trinket or two to satisfy them. Something you might have given me and something I might have stolen if I were left alone for a moment."

He laughed, but his laughter was grim. No one in Ilium knew when Odysseus entered the City a few nights later. I learned later that he and Diomedes had scaled the city walls at a place so steep and forbidding that it was carelessly guarded. But he left by the gate he had entered as a beggar, and every guard on duty was left with his throat neatly slit and his blood draining into the thirsty dust.

I suppose that of all the days I spent in Ilium the days that followed were the hardest. We knew that things were coming to an end, but not when or how. We were sure that Odysseus had been successful in stealing the wooden statue on which the safety of the City depended, and almost sure that the priestess of Athena knew that it was gone. Aethra said that she seemed to have aged years overnight and looked like a dying woman. So far as we could tell, the priestess had been afraid to tell Priam of the loss, but we now had so little contact with the royal family that we could not be sure.

The truce which had been called for the funeral rites of Achilles seemed to go on and on, and there were rumors of strife in the Argive camp: perhaps even mutiny. Spies who had slipped as close to the camp as they dared brought back stories of seeing a gigantic Argive fighting with his comrades in arms: we suspected, but did not know until later that the man was Ajax. The time the truce would normally have been over was long past and the Argives did not launch an attack, as they normally did after a truce. Spies brought back stories of activity around the ships and hope soared in the City.

Then the day came when we heard a tumult in the streets and among the shouts and cries and snatches of song we heard someone shouting over and over, "They're gone! The Argives are gone!" My heart gave a bound, then suddenly I realized what this meant. Odysseus was putting his plan into operation and the life of the City was numbered in days at the most. My Lady turned to me and said, "We need to know what is happening, M'pha. Borrow some clothing from one of the servants and go out into the streets. Talk to the merchants and servants; word gets to them as quickly as it does to anyone. If you can find Phyrgos send him to me. As soon as the gates are open I'm going to send him out of the City in charge of all our servants and all of the others I can persuade to go." There would be many of those, I knew; My Lady had quietly helped a good many of the victims of the war, widows and orphans and men crippled in the fighting: whatever the nobles thought of her she was popular among the poor folk of the City.

My Lady looked me in the eyes and said quietly, "I suppose you wouldn't go with them, even if I commanded you to?" I shook my head and she smiled. "That mysterious promise you made? Or is that just an excuse for being loyal? All right, M'pha. I think you and I and Aethra will be as safe as anyone can be in a city being sacked. The Spartans will rally to me, the Athenians to Aethra and the Cretans to you: between the three contingents someone should reach us in time to fend off the freelance looters and rapists. All right, go now and find out what you can."

Going out into the streets, I felt like a recently widowed woman obliged to attend some great and joyous feast, trying not to spoil the joy of others but unable to forget her own sorrow. When I got to the gates I found a milling crowd; the wildest rumors were being passed from mouth to mouth. Eventually I found that all anyone knew for sure was that a strong force of City troops under Deiphobus had been

117

sent out; they would make their way to the Argive camp to find out if the enemy had actually left, but they were prepared to fight if this was a trick or ambush. Then I had a stroke of luck: the gates were opened to admit a small contingent of City warriors and I saw Phyrgos among them. I called his name at the top of my lungs and he came over to me.

"Well, they're really gone, my Lady," he said with a grin. "We caught one Argive skulking in the ruins of the camp and he was questioned pretty roughly. According to this man, Ajax, the giant from Salamis, ran mad and killed quite a few Argives before they brought him down. Then their soothsayers were consulted and told Agamemnon that the gods had turned against the Argives and there would be nothing but sorrow and defeat for them if they stayed. So they're off to their homes, hoping to raid every small city they pass on the way and come home with something to show for their ten years...."

Phyrgos was so big and shaggy that it was easy to forget that he was no fool. I had not guarded my reactions carefully enough and suddenly I was aware that the shrewd eyes under those shaggy brows were searching my face.

"I think you know something, little lady," he said in his rumbling voice. "And seeing how you took it woke up my own doubts. It's all a little too easy, isn't it? I thought that Argive was a coward, but perhaps he's a very brave man. Some hot heads were talking about cutting off his nose and ears when I left. Not a fighter's thing to do, taking out your wrongs on a captive. Lord Hector would never have allowed it.... Does Lady Helen need me?"

"She wants you to take a party out of the City fairiy soon," I said in a low voice. "If I were you I'd tell my family and friends to pack up a few possessions and go along with you."

There was a flicker in the eyes of the grizzled warrior, but his face was impassive. "Ah, so that's the way of it," he said softly. "Well, I won't be sorry to get out of this city after ten years. No doubt Lady Helen would like some of us to go to Lord Paris's old estate up on the slopes of Ida and see what we can salvage from the crops that have been left unharvested up there during the war?"

"I think that's a very good idea," I told him. "My Lady will be glad to give a share of the food to any of the poor folk who go out to help gather the crops. You might pass the word."

Phyrgos nodded, his face still impassive, then gave me a salute and moved off. Then he paused and turned. "I think they'll let the people from the City go down to the shore soon," he said. "If you have a chance, go. There's something down there of a kind you're not likely to see again. The Argives have used some of their wrecked ships to build a great wooden horse and dedicated it to the Gray-eyed Lady. The thing is almost as tall as the walls."

Phyrgos was right: as soon as it was apparent that no sizable body of Argives could be hidden anywhere nearby Deiphobus ordered the gates of the City flung open so that all the people of the city could go down and gape at the ruins of the Argive camp. They streamed out of the gates in a festival mood, shouting and singing and drinking from skins of wine which were being passed around. I followed along the fringes of the crowd with some of the fishwives from the market. I would be safe from any boisterous reveler in their company; they were well known for the strength of their arms and the sharpness of their tongues.

They were a merry group, calling back and forth

jokes about the mess the Argives had left behind when they broke camp. "Well what do you expect?" cried one woman. "All those men pigging it here with only a few captive girls to look after them, and they'll have been kept too busy to do much housecleaning." This was greeted with a burst of ribald laughter, but suddenly this died away as we came around a little hillock and saw the Horse for the first time.

It towered high in the sky on four tremendous spars which were anchored to a platform strongly constructed of massive planks. On the platform was a small altar, still wet with the blood of sacrifices. The body of the thing seemed to be made of at least two ships, one upside down on top of the other, bound together by ropes passed round and round them. A great mass of pieces of rope at the stem end suggested a tail, and at the bow end of the ships another massive spar had been fixed, with short pieces of rope along it to suggest a mane.

The "head" consisted of two small fishing boats, fastened together as the two ships which composed the "body" were, but they had been propped apart at one end so that the head had a gaping "mouth" which seemed to grin obscenely. The paddles of two steering oars formed the ears and great staring eyes had been painted on the head.

Starting a little above the platform the whole creation had been heavily tarred: the legs, the body, the head even the ropes of the mane and tail were black and shining and sticky with tar: the pungent tang of it filled your nostrils as you approached the thing.

I do not know who first suggested moving the Horse to the walls of the City. There were plenty of rollers lying around, which had been used to draw up the Argive ships on the shore, and a great deal of rope in odd lengths, knotted and worn. Once the idea of moving the thing caught the fancy of the mob they worked as if they were a work gang under the lash of some harsh overseer. Some of the people manhandled rollers in front of the platform on which the Horse was based; others began knotting the ropes together and hunting for heavy sticks to use as levers.

As they actually got the thing moving the pace grew even more frenzied. Pairs of men carrying rollers which the Horse had already passed over were actually running as they carried the rollers up to the front of the Horse again. People were fighting for a hold on the ropes pulling the Horse and poking at each other to clear a space in which they might apply their levers. The sight of the great Horse lurching and rattling over the plain which had seen so many bloody battles was grotesque yet at the same time awesome: it was as if some giant horse out of a fevered dream were trampling through the crowd as it raced to the City.

I took no part in moving the horse myself, but I could not tear myself away from the spectacle of its being moved. Only when we reached the walls and the crowd swarmed up the stairways to tear away the superstructure of the gate so that the Horse could be moved into the City itself was I able to start for the House of the Golden Lintel. There was something unnatural about the way in which the crowd's frenzy had resulted in this swift concerted action. I could almost feel the Olympian presence around me and I looked in horrified fascination at the ringleaders of the crowd, wondering if one of them was an Olympian hid under a disguise of illusion.

I had gone a few steps into the City when I saw Cassandra coming toward me, her hair loose and tangled, her feet bare, her eyes staring. There was a frenzy in her which matched the frenzy of the crowd, and for a moment they stopped and gaped at her as she railed at them: "Fools, fools, fools! Put the torch to that accursed thing! Don't you know that it's full of Argive soldiers, come to destroy the City!"

Chapter Nine

THE VOICES

For a moment she almost swayed the crowd, such was the force of her conviction. But then a coarse voice from the crowd called out, "Just because you had a belly full of Argives doesn't mean horsie here does'" and the crowd laughed and hooted. Cassandra had come back pregnant from one of the Harvest Festivals, and since no man of the City would have dared to lay a finger on her it was immediately whispered that the father must be an Argive. When she was delivered of twins everyone claimed to recognize the babies as plainly having Argive features, though to me they looked just like any other babies. The incident had done much to destroy any respect or credibility Cassandra might have had, and when the coarse voice reminded the crowd of it, Cassandra's words were drowned out with hoots and laughter.

I was looking at the body of the Horse wondering if it could actually be hiding a group of Argives. That body was made up of the hulls of two ships: there would certainly be room for at least as many men as a ship normally held, perhaps more if some kind of platform was rigged between the upper and lower ship hulls. The massive spars that made up the legs of the Horse would certainly bear the weight, indeed the way they were splayed out made it likely that they had been designed to bear a greater weight than that of empty hulls. The lavish covering of tar on the horse made it impossible to climb up to the body, as some daredevils would have been sure to do if the wood had been left bare. I began to be more and more sure that Cassandra was right, despite that powerful impulse to disbelieve any of her prophecies.

I opened my mouth to speak, then shut it again. If

there were Argives in the Horse this must be the scheme Odysseus had spoken of to get an advance guard of Argives into the City. That the Argives should take the City was what my Lady wanted and what I wanted—or was it? Argives in the City looting, killing people I had lived with for all these years, leading others away captive... I opened my mouth to speak but another voice, loud and self-assured spoke first.

"I am Laocoon, the seer," a stout, richly dressed man was saying. "Even a madwoman may be right by accident. In this case she is—my gifts tell me that if you bring this Horse within the walls disaster will come to the City. Give me a torch, you there by the guardroom: I will burn this thing myself and save the City!"

So fickle is a crowd that for a moment they were all with him and men ran for torches to burn the Horse. But suddenly there were gasps and shouts from the crowd: two immense serpents had appeared from nowhere and were heading straight for Laocoon. In an instant he was entangled in their coils and his shouts had turned to screams of agony. Two young men came out of the crowd, which had shrunk back in horror. "Father! Father!" they cried and tried to pry the serpents' coils from the stricken man. But soon they too were entangled and screaming in their turn. No one dared to go to their rescue after what had happened: it was plain that these were not ordinary serpents, but some sending of the Olympians. I turned away, sickened, from the dying men: plainly the same Olympian powers which had impelled the frenzied mob to haul the Horse into the City would deal ruthlessly with any attempts to interfere.

When I made my way back to the House of the Golden Lintel and told my Lady what had happened she sat for a long time looking into the fire, then sighed and said:

"I fear that this is the last night for the City, M'pha. If there are Argives in that Horse they can hardly plan to spend more than one night there. Make sure all of our servants and their families are on their way out of the City, then lock the doors and make sure no light shows in the house tonight. Those who come for me will not be put off by locked doors, but casual looters may look for places that show more signs of occupation."

By evening everyone we could command or persuade was out of the City and my Lady, Aethra and I were sitting by a low fire on the hearth in the Great Hall. There was a thundrous knocking on the door and I looked at my Lady. She shook her head. "Too early for Argive raiders," she said. "They'll attack in the dark hours before dawn, if I know them. Listen by the door, M'pha, and use your judgment as to whether to open it."

When I got to the door I heard Deiphobus's voice bawling outside, demanding entrance. When it was plain that he would break in the door if we did not open it, I reluctantly unbarred the door and let him in. He was wild-eyed and had a drawn sword in his hand. "Bring me to Helen," he rapped out. I had no choice but to obey, but I kept my hand on the dagger I wore under my robe in case looters broke in.

When we came into the Hall I half feared that he would attack my mistress and eased my dagger in its sheath, but he stood before her glowering, and began to speak. "I'm your husband, at least in name, Lady Helen; much good it's done me. But in this at least I demand your wifely obedience. I've heard of Cassandra's prophecy and what happened to Laocoon: I've no doubt they were both right. I'd be mobbed if I tried to burn the horse, but I have a plan to lure the Argives out of it. Then the people will have to believe! Come with me, Helen, I demand it!"

Lady Helen shrugged delicately: her movements were as graceful as ever. She took a cloak that was in readiness by her chair and put it over her shoulders. I grabbed my own cloak and put it on; I was not going to be left behind. Aethra half rose, but my Lady shook her head. "Stay in charge of the house. Lady Aethra," she said. Then she drew a veil over her head and followed Deiphobus from the house, and I followed her.

As we walked along the streets of the City we saw small rejoicing groups but the streets were emptier than I expected, and I hoped that my Lady's efforts to get people out of the City had been of some use. But there were so many people here still, so many who would suffer when the Argives took the City....

When we arrived at the open space inside the Scaean Gate where the Horse stood we found a quiet circle of people gazing at it, not talking or moving around much but simply standing and staring, awe-struck, at the enormous structure. Deiphobus was right: any attempt to simply destroy the thing would rouse the crowd, even if it were done by a member of the royal family. But if the crowd actually saw an Argive come out of the Horse their mood would change: the gigantic creation would be burned or overturned in a few moments. How did Deiphobus hope to make the Argives reveal their presence?

We soon found out. Deiphobus led us through the crowd into the open space which surrounded the Horse and stopped. The pungent smell of tar filled my nostrils and the giant creature towered above us ominously against the darkening sky. Deiphobus turned and faced Helen. "I've heard you, when Paris was alive, imitate the voices of some of the Argive queens: your sister Clytemnestra, Odysseus's wife, some of the others. If there are Argives in that thing some of their leaders will be there. Speak to them in their wives' voices: one of them may be fool enough to betray himself. It's the best plan I can think of, and it may be our last chance. Do it or I'll slay you here on the spot as a traitor to the City."

My Lady looked at him in silence for a moment, then gave that delicate shrug again. I was having a hard time keeping silence. Traitor to the City indeed! What allegiance did Lady Helen owe the City, what had the folk of Ilium done for her? Paris had taken her from her home and brought her here and except for a few of larger mind and soul like Hector, the people of the City had alternately cursed her and gaped at her as if she were some work of art displayed to honor the gods and adorn the City.

Lady Helen lifted her head to look at the Horse, and through the veil I could see in the dying light a little smile playing about her lips. "Menelaus!" she called. "Come down and rescue me! They've married me to Deiphobus and he's threatening to kill me!" Then she called again in a voice deeper and richer than her own. "Odysseus! Come down, come down! The Trojans have sent out raiders to capture the Argive queens! If you don't rescue us, they'll kill us out of revenge for the Trojans you've slain!"

"Good, good," said Deiphobus in a low voice. "Keep on! One of them is sure to betray himself." I could have laughed out loud; Menelaus and Odysseus knew as well as Deiphobus did Lady Helen's trick of mimicking voices. Once they had heard her voice they would know that any others they heard must be her mimicry.

"Agamemnon!" cried out Helen in a sharper voice,

127

with a Spartan twang even more pronounced. "Get down here! How dare you let your wife be treated this way! Do you call yourself a man? Come down at once!" This was pure fun on my Lady's part; she knew well that however Agamemnon blustered in Council as "King of Men" and "High King," at home he was the victim of Clytemnestra's sharp tongue.

My Lady was enjoying herself now, remembering all the Argive ladies she had met as Queen of Sparta and using their voices to poke fun at their husbands' foibles. Once when she called out in the voice of Aglaia, the wife of Arriclus, a minor noble from the Islands, I thought I heard a stirring from above us. Deiphobus gestured frantically for silence and Lady Helen obeyed, but after that brief scuffling sound we heard no more. Deiphobus gestured for my Lady to continue, but eventually when she began to hesitate, unable to remember more voices, he had to admit defeat.

"All right," he growled. "You've done what I told you and it hasn't worked. All I can do now is try to find enough men who haven't drunk themselves useless to mount a guard over this thing." He lurched away, leaving us standing by the Horse. It was not fitting for him to leave my Lady without his escort, but I was glad to see the last of him. When I contrasted his present brusqueness with his flattering ways before my Lady had lost her beauty it was hard to have any patience with him.

The gates were still partly open, though they would be closed and guarded when it grew full dark. My Lady gestured to me and we walked over to the gates and stepped outside. The plains outside the City which had for so long been the field of battle were eery in the half light and the hair rose on the back of my neck as I saw figures moving on the plains. Surely fear of slain men's ghosts would keep even the hardiest scavenger off that plain in the half dark!

My Lady moved a little farther from the gate and gave a low call. A figure ran lightly toward us from the same hillock Ajax had hidden behind on the day Achilles had died, and with a little ripple of fear I saw that it was Oenone, the Wild Girl I had met that day. She ran lightly up to us and regarded us with the frank curiosity of a child. When she spoke it was to me. "Did Alexander die then?" she asked placidly. At my nod she gave a little shrug and looked around the plain. "They aren't fighting anymore," she said, "and the Northern Men have gone away. But still the people stay huddled in the Mountain of Houses."

My Lady put back her veil and looked into the eyes of the Wild Girl. "Oenone," she said softly. "Your people are wandering on the plain. Why not lead them into the Mountain of Houses, let them wander the streets and send the Call. Perhaps many of the people might follow you out into the wilds."

The Wild Girl put her head on one side and considered. "Yes, we could do that," she said. "Perhaps they'd come and worship at the Grove as they did in the old days. We haven't had anyone at the Grove for the festivals for many summers.... Yes, we'll do it." Her eyes searched my Lady's face for a moment and she said, "You've changed." I felt a little pang for Lady Helen but she went on. "You used to be like Aphrodite, but now you remind me of Demeter." With a little bob of her head that was almost a gesture of homage the Wild Girl turned and ran lightly away.

"That may get a few more out of the City," said my Lady. "Perhaps quite a few." She passed her hand over her forehead in a gesture of weariness, and let down her veil again. "I wonder what she meant about Demeter? Well, she lost her daughter once and I've been separated from mine for ten long years. I wonder if Menelaus has had any news of my Hermione.... Well, let's go back to the house, M'pha. Aethra will be wondering what's happened to us."

As we walked back through silent streets I pondered the Wild Girl's words. Demeter was the Lady of the Great Mystery at Eleusis: what initiates learned there gave them strength to face the sorrows of mortality. How had Helen grown like Demeter? Perhaps, I thought, because she had grown in compassion. Ten years ago my Lady would not have worried about the fate of the poor folk of the City. Even as short a time ago as the incident of Penthesileia I had been thinking of Lady Helen as still being what she used to be, but she had grown and changed. What would Menelaus make of the new Helen? Well, we would soon have a chance to find out.

Chapter Ten

THE PARTING

It was a long, weary night for of course we did not dare go to bed. We sat in the darkened Hall and listened to ambiguous voices from the streets outside. Once or twice there were shouts or sounds of feet outside, but they died away and no one tried to enter the House of the Golden Lintel. But at last there was a crash from the door, someone without bothering to knock had simply smashed in the door. My Lady put her veil over her head and stood up: Aethra and I left our chairs to stand beside her.

The door to the Hall was dashed open and a single Argive in bronze armor stood there: not a common soldier but not one of the Argive leaders either. His helmet was askew and its horsehair plume bedraggled; his face looked as if he had been drinking. There was blood on his hands and patches of something black on his arms and legs. Suddenly I realized it was pitch: there had been men in the Horse and this man must have been one of them!

"Three women," the man said in a slurred voice. "Well, now, aren't I lucky. Which one of you is going to be lucky first?" he asked with a leer. I was wishing for my net and trident: with them I could easily have handled this drunken fool. Perhaps if I went to him with a show of willingness I'd have a chance to use my dagger.... But already there were sounds of other feet coming in the shattered front door. The drunken Argive wheeled. "Go on, you sons of Trojans, get out of here!" he shouted. "Find your own goodies, these are mine!"

He was shouldered aside by a big man whom I recognized with a stab of joy as the Spartan captain who had spoken to me in the garden of Apollo's temple. Ignoring the drunken warrior, the Spartan gave Helen the royal salute and said in his deep voice, "At your service, my Queen."

"It is good to see you, Merionathes," said my Lady calmly. "Did the king take any hurt in the battle?"

"No, my Lady," the Spartan began, when he was interrupted by an indignant squawk from the man who had entered first. Merionathes turned and put his formidable visage close to the other man's face. "Keep silent when your betters are speaking, fellow," he said grimly. "Behave yourself and I'll let you go with one of my men to tell King Menelaus that Queen Helen has been found safe and unharmed. But if you'd rather have trouble than a rich reward from the King, I'll be glad to oblige."

Half sobered by fear, the man let Merionathes push him out of the room. Lady Helen resumed her seat and Aethra and I did likewise. Merionathes removed his helmet and bowed gravely before he continued his interrupted speech. "The King, my Lady, is well and so was Princess Hermione last news we had from home. I hear she is growing up very like her mother, my Lady...."

There were voices from the hall and Merionathes stepped outside and saluted as Menelaus himself came into the room. Like the man who had entered first, Menelaus had splashes of tar on his arms and legs: he too must have been in the Horse. He seemed unwounded, but there was blood on the drawn sword in his hand.

"I'll see to the guards," murmured Merionathes tactfully, and stepped outside the door, pulling it closed behind him. Menelaus tugged off his helmet and let it fall to the floor with a weary gesture. His red hair was dark with sweat and matted on his brow: there were threads of silver in it.

"Deiphobus's blood is on this sword," he said harshly. His face was flushed, but not with wine: could he be embarrassed, I wondered?

"Deiphobus didn't matter," said Lady Helen, standing and taking a step toward her husband. She put her veil back from her face and said quietly. "It was a marriage in form only: you can see why. Aphrodite and I had a falling out." When Menelaus said nothing, she kept on talking, her eyes on his face. "It did matter when you beat Paris in your single battle with him," she said. "If it hadn't been for Aphrodite that would have ended the war then. I wish it had."

"Paris didn't matter either," said Menelaus. "Not if you...." Suddenly there was a commotion in the hall and a big arrogant man in splendid armor pushed his way into the room. It was Agamemnon of course, pushing his way into this moment that should have belonged to Helen and Menelaus alone, as he had pushed his way into their relationship before Helen had left Sparta.

"You all right, youngster?" he asked Menelaus patronizingly. "Hot work out there." He himself showed no signs of having fought: Agamemnon was one to lead from the rear. His eyes searched the room, then fastened on my Lady. "I heard they'd found Helen so I came... Great Zeus, is this her? Lost her looks, has she? Might as well avenge your honor by putting her to the sword, brother: no use showing this to the army as the reason for ten years of fighting." Menelaus lifted his sword, but not to strike Helen: for a moment I thought he would cut down Agamemnon, who stood arrogantly unconscious that his suggestion could be in any way offensive to his younger brother.

Richard Purtill

"We'd have to think of a regent, then, tall Princess Hermione comes of age to marry," said Merionathes, who had entered behind Agamemnon. "And I doubt if Argives will be very popular in Sparta when the word gets out that you've killed the queen." His voice was outwardly respectful but I could tell he was as outraged as I was. He had kept his head, though: while outright opposition would have only made Agamemnon stubborn, this reminder that his brother only held the throne of Sparta by marriage to Helen evidently gave him pause. He opened his mouth to speak, but a deep smooth voice cut in from behind him.

"No need to frighten Queen Helen with talk of killing, I'm sure she's repentant enough already," said Odysseus smoothly. "No doubt she longs for the sisterly consolation your queen will give her when we return home." Odysseus was almost as grotesque a figure as he had been when he had played beggar, covered with blood and with pitch from the Horse, but I could have run over and hugged, him. Helen gave him a little smile and their eyes met: for a moment I had the feeling that two adults were smiling at the squabbles of children. My heart stopped pounding and I drew a deep breath. With Odysseus here to maneuver Agamemnon my Lady was in no danger: the "King of Men" had just been reminded that his wife was the sister of the woman whom he had so casually proposed killing and would make his life miserable if he did any such thing.

"They've opened Priam's treasure house, my King," Odysseus went on. "There are some remarkable things, if you'd like to see...." A gleam came into Agamemnon's eyes and he turned hastily to go.

"Oh well, do as you like, brother," he said to Menelaus. "She's your wife after all. But keep a veil on her

134

if you don't want us to be a laughing stock. By the Three
Kings Clytemnestra is the better favored now. How she'll
rejoice at that!" He shouldered his way out of the room and I
sent the wish after him that someone report that last remark
to his wife.

Odysseus smiled as he left and said to Menelaus, "I'll
keep him out of your way for a while, my friend. Don't hold it
too much against him; he is what he is." He turned to myself
and Aethra. "Lady Aethra, there are some of the Athenians
waiting to escort you to suitable quarters; Lady M'pha, Prince
Idomeneus is waiting for you outside the house. Let's leave
husband and wife alone together; they'll have much to talk
of." As he ushered us out he turned to Helen and said quietly,
"You know what we owe you. Queen Helen. Command me
if I can do you any service. Blessings on both of you." For
once, I think the sincerity in that marvelous voice of his was
genuine.

Before I left the room I turned to look at Helen and
Menelaus. I would see her again, no doubt but I was no
longer her lady in waiting; the promise I had made long ago
to my mother was fulfilled. I had stayed with Helen through
all her troubles until she was back with Menelaus. These
troubles had been longer and darker than my mother or I had
suspected when I made that promise, but I was not sorry that
I had kept faith to the end. Her eyes were on Menelaus and
I doubt if she saw me, but before I left the room I gave for
one last time the salute to her as my Lady and mistress, my
Lady Helen.

BOOK THREE

Menelaus

BOOK THREE: Menelaus

Chapter One
INSIDE

For what seemed the hundredth time, I removed Diomedes's foot from my shoulder. I glanced upward and in the few rays of light that found their way into our hiding place I saw the big man grin apologetically. I raised my hand and grinned back. There was no real malice in Diomedes. If you were on the other side in a battle he would kill you, cheerfully and efficiently. Even if you were on his side he would kill you if Odysseus told him to, or if he thought you were a threat to Odysseus. I counted the wily Ithakan as my best friend and would have done a great deal for him, but Diomedes was more than a friend to Odysseus: he was his shield and his right hand. That was why Diomedes rather than Odysseus was next in line after me: when we came down the ladders Diomedes would clear the way for Odysseus.

I shifted my weight and tried to make myself a little more comfortable on the netting on which we lay. The netting had been a stroke of genius: without it we would have rattled around like seeds in a dried gourd when they had pulled us up from the beach. And it meant that there could be two layers of us inside the hulls, though that was a very mixed blessing. Some of the men in the upper net had been sick when they had moved us, and the smell of vomit mixed with the smell of urine and the overwhelming stench of tar.

I shut my eyes and tried to forget my surroundings and think of something else. Diomedes and Odysseus, since my attention had been called to them, would do as well as anything. Not so many nights ago I thought I had witnessed a portent, a falling out between the two. They had come back to camp from their midnight raid on Troy; Diomedes was carrying something wrapped in a cloak and with a drawn sword in his hand was forcing a very angry Odysseus to go ahead of him. It looked as if they had had a falling out over the booty they had gone to fetch, and so they had, though not quite in the way it appeared.

When Diomedes saw me he had saluted with his sword and said quietly, "My Lord, will you give orders for this thing to be held in a safe place with a guard of steady men over it? I'll put it there myself: the fewer that touch it or even see it the better. This is a holy thing belonging to the Gray-eyed Lady and anyone who has dealings with it is likely to incur her wrath...."

Odysseus broke in angrily, "And who was it told you that, you great ox? If you'd let me take it there'd have been no trouble: Athena isn't likely to turn on me after all these years." It was true enough that the Ithakan king had always been a favorite of Athena's: time after time she had helped him in battle or council.

Diomedes shrugged. "Well, she's helped me often enough for your sake or my own," he told Odysseus. "If her favorites are safe then I'm as likely to be safe as you. But you know as well as I that the Olympians can turn against you in a minute. She didn't tell us about this thing I'm carrying, you ferreted it out yourself. And if it's so safe to handle it why did you strictly forbid me to put a finger on it? I'm not a fool, even if I don't have your wits!"

Odysseus growled at him but Diomedes was quite right: he was no fool and for once he had outwitted his companion. Odysseus had forgotten that Diomedes would do anything for him except harm him or let him be harmed. In warning Diomedes, Odysseus had alerted him to a danger, and the big man had taken the danger on himself as he always would if given a chance.

Thinking of that scene I felt a sudden sharp loneliness. There was no one in the world as close to me as Diomedes was to Odysseus: no one who would disobey orders and take a danger on himself rather than let it fall on me. For all his protestations of devotion to me and to my interests I knew that my brother regarded me as a pawn and a puppet: thought of my kingdom as only an extension of his and of myself as one of his less valuable subordinates. There was only one person I had thought for a while really loved me and she....

Suddenly I heard it, her voice, clear and strong. "Menelaus," she called from below, "Menelaus, come down and rescue me! They've married me to Deiphobus, and he's threatening to kill me!" If I had been on a solid surface I would probably have sprung to my feet and rushed to the fastenings of the trapdoor, but while I was trying to heave myself up from where I was sprawled on the nets I felt the touch of a spear-butt on my cheek and I looked up to see Odysseus shaking his head.

I began to think again as the surge of blind rage subsided. I knew that Helen was here, I even knew that the Trojans had given her to Deiphobus. But why should they try to kill her unless . . .of course! Deiphobus suspected that we were up here and was using Helen to try to make us betray ourselves. He wouldn't really hurt her, no one could look at that face and do her harm.... But if I heard her scream could I contain myself?

She didn't scream: the next time I heard her voice she was imitating Penelope. "Odysseus, Odysseus, come down!"

she cried. "The Trojans have sent out raiders to capture the Argive queens! If you don't rescue us, they'll kill us out of revenge for the Trojans you've slain!" I was still looking up at Odysseus and saw his face twist with pain at the sound of that voice so like his wife's: the Ithakan king was devoted to plain little Penelope. And she to him; suddenly I realized that Penelope would let herself be killed gladly rather than lure her husband into a trap.

With a curious lightening of my heart I realized that Helen was not really trying to fool us. "Deiphobus is threatening to kill me;" that was her way of telling us that she was being forced to act out his part. And she knew as well as I that, good mimic though she was, she could never fool Odysseus into thinking that her voice was Penelope's or that Penelope would say those words. When I heard the murmur of a man's voice below I pictured a band of armed Trojans waiting for us to betray ourselves. I put my finger to my lips and gestured to Odysseus to pass the signal on to the others. He nodded and touched the foot of the man beyond him.

I jumped a little as I heard the harsh tones of Helen's sister and my sister-in-law, Clytemnestra, "Agamemnon! Get down here! How dare you let your wife be treated this way! Do you call yourself a man? Come down at once!" The ropes of the netting trembled as Diomedes shook with silent laughter and I too relaxed and smiled after a moment. Helen's imitation of Clystemnestra was uncharitably accurate: anyone who had known the "King of Men" and his spouse would recognize the accuracy of her portrayal. Whatever else she had done Helen had never used that tone of contempt to me. Her sister hardly spoke to Agamemnon in any other tone. Perhaps despite everything my marriage had been luckier than his.

Once it was clear what Helen was doing, most of us simply relaxed and enjoyed the performance, but there is always some fool who does not understand what is going on. In response to one of Helen's imitations a man named Articlus tried to climb down the nets: the poor fool must have been fond of his wife and believed that the voice was actually hers. He was stopped quickly and ruthlessly before he could betray us all: I saw to it later that he had an honorable funeral with the others who fought and died.

Eventually Helen ran out of voices to imitate. I heard the murmur of male voices again and footsteps going away, but I did not feel that we had been left alone: I felt presences around us. But there were no more voices until after long hours I heard a strange undulating call. Surely no human throat had made that noise! I felt a sudden longing to be out in the fresh air, out in the open, away from buildings, away from other people. I felt as if I were shut in a dark stinking box that was closing in on me and I bit my lips and clenched my nails into my palms in an effort to keep from bursting out of my confinement.

"Cover your ears," said the low, deep voice of Odysseus. Quick-witted, he must have weighed the danger of speaking against the danger of keeping silent and decided to take the risk of speaking. I jammed my fingers into my ears and tried to listen only to the sound of my own heartbeat. When finally I dared to take my fingers out there was deep silence again and I no longer felt the sense of any presence around us. I touched Diomedes's foot and he touched Odysseus. There was a little pause and then Odysseus spoke one word: "Yes."

I rolled out of the net onto the boards below me. With

the weighted pommel of my dagger I knocked out the pin and the trapdoor crashed open. I kicked the rope ladder out and was swarming down it almost before its end had hit the ground below. This was the moment of greatest danger: if there were archers below they could pick us off one by one as we descended those ladders.

My feet touched the ground and I whirled around in a fighting crouch, my light shield raised against missiles and my sword in my hand. But all around me was dark and silent and one after another my companions swarmed down the ladders and formed up in a circle around the Horse.

We were in a little paved courtyard just inside the Scaean Gate. The gates were closed and barred but there was no sign of the guard that should have turned out at the noise we had made. I drew a breath and tried to remember the plans Odysseus and I had discussed. They were his plans of course, but I would give the orders and Odysseus would listen to his own ideas from my mouth with respectful attention. It was one of the things I loved him for: he was always building up my authority just as my brother was always tearing it down.

"King Odysseus, take a party along the walls, eliminate any sentries who might give the alarm," I said. "Prince Idomeneus, your men should open the gates as quietly as you can, then disable them so that they can't be closed again. The rest of you with me: we get as high up the hill as we can before we're seen, then light a beacon to call the main army in. If we're hard pressed by an unexpected attack remember that a good fire is of more immediate use than any number of dead Trojans: fight them off and put a torch to whatever will burn. Let's go!"

There were sleeping folk on the edge of the square: I don't know if they were drunk from "victory" celebrations or whether some Olympian had cast a sleep on them. We ignored them and went up the steep streets at a trot, a formidable force but pitifully few if any sizable force of Trojans turned out.

At first, the opposition was scattered and we easily killed the few Trojans who were foolish enough to challenge us. But as we drew nearer to Priam's palace there were signs of more organized resistance: a little group of archers on a roof and then a line of warriors across the street who looked as if they were meant to delay us while troops massed behind. I signaled our troops to a halt and turned to my second in command.

"We don't want those archers behind us, Merionathes," I told him. "And the house they're on has quite a bit of wood in it. Kill two hares with one arrow: get those archers and then set fire to the house as you come down again. You can see over the walls from here so our army will see the fire." Merionathes and his men saluted and moved off: they knew as well as I did that some of them would die getting up on that roof, but they were Spartans and would have obeyed as readily if I had told them to fire the house and remain in it.

I saw no point in going forward to meet the screen of Trojan warriors until Merionathes had removed the threat of the archers, so I told my men to stand easy and see to their gear. The Trojans stood their ground, staring at us: we must have seemed figures out of a nightmare to them, suddenly appearing on the night after they thought they had won their war.

The main body of Trojans for which the screen of troops had been waiting appeared from farther up the street just as flames shot up from the roof where the archers had been. There was no great point in fighting the larger force now that our main objective had been accomplished, but my blood was up and we needed at least to fight a rear-guard action until Merionathes and what remained of his men could get clear of the burning house. I raised the war cry and charged their line, my men running a pace or two behind me.

We took their first line unawares: no doubt they expected our small force to run back instead of forward when we saw their main body of troops. We ran over them and left them smashed and dying behind us, then fought our way into the main body of troops until we were stopped by sheer press of numbers.

We could have died right there, but the apparently formidable Trojan force was half drunk and half armed. Beyond that there was something in their souls and in ours: both of us knew that Troy had fallen and sooner or later they were dead men. If they survived this battle they would only die in another. But every one of my men was filled with a fierce determination not to die in this last battle but to live to reap the harvest of victory.

Some of us died, but more of them. Presently the street was clear in front of me and I turned around to see Merionathes, grinning, at my elbow. He pointed with his sword at the now towering flame from the house he had fired. "That will bring the army in," he said. "All we have to do is stay in one piece until they get here."

But even as he spoke I heard the sounds of an even larger force coming down from the citadel above: the clatter of armor, the sound of marching feet, the rattle of chariots and the hoofbeats of the great war-horses which drew them.

Chapter Two

THE MEETING

The horses were a mistake: in the city streets they had no room to turn and could only charge straight ahead. As soon as I heard the hooves I gave orders to collect burning brands from the house, which was now blazing fiercely. A few brave men volunteered to run at the chariot horses with torches in their hands; others stood back and threw torches or shot burning arrows from their bows. The horses panicked, of course, reared up and broke their traces, leaving the chariots neatly blocking the street. A few of my men were trampled and one was killed when a rearing horse struck out with a forefoot, but we did far more damage to the Trojans: throwing their ranks into disarray with arrows, thrown spears and flung torches.

Soon enough, someone took charge, ordered the main body of troops to fall back and regroup and gathered a little band of heavily armed warriors to rush the barricade made by the wrecked chariots. I saw with grim satisfaction that several of the men had richly decorated armor; they were men of note and perhaps even sons of Priam. There was one son of Priam I very much wanted to meet.

The gods granted my wish: when a band of Trojans had fought their way past the chariots, one stood back a little and cried out, "I am Deiphobus, Priam's son! If Menelaus is there let him come forth and face me!" I stepped forward and gave him his chance to make a mockery of our purpose in coming to storm Troy by killing me before I could reclaim Helen. I am no Achilles, but then neither was he. The battle was short and sharp and ended with my sword in his guts just under his bronze corselet.

147

He lay on the littered street, bleeding out his life, and looked up at me with eyes full of hate, "Go claim your woman, Menelaus," he gasped. "Much joy may you have of her." He began to laugh, a dreadful, choking laugh, and laughing he died. What did he mean? If they had harmed Helen.... I turned to fling myself on the Trojan ranks but suddenly there was one of my Spartans at my shoulder saying urgently, "Queen Helen has been found, my Lord, safe and sound. Merionathes is with her...." For a moment I could hardly breathe for the mixture of emotions that surged up within me, and then I was striding through deserted side streets while the noise of battle died behind me.

There was another man leading the way along with my man: this fellow was not a Spartan but from his accent one of the Myrmidons who had followed Achilles. He was babbling something about being the first to find Helen and being promised a reward. I told him curtly that he'd be seen to in good time, to seek me out after the battle was over. The man seemed put out and dropped a little behind; when I looked around a little later he was gone. I shrugged and forgot him: I'd reward him generously enough if he survived the fighting, but I knew well enough he'd probably found Helen by foraging for loot instead of staying with his comrades and fighting. Had he been in the Horse? I couldn't remember; if he hadn't it meant that the main force was already inside Troy.

Sooner than I expected we were standing before an ornate house high on the central hill of Troy, just below Priam's palace. The fighting was below us now: we had come around the battle and passed it by. The door of the house had been smashed in, probably by the looter, but when I pushed it open, a little band of Spartans faced me with menace, turning respectful when they saw who I was. "Merionathes is in the Hall with the Queen," said one of the men and he opened the door for me.

I heard Merionathes's voice saying something about seeing to the guard, and was aware of him slipping past me. But I had no eyes for anything but a slender veiled figure standing a spear's cast away from me. There were other women beside her; Aethra looking very little changed and the Cretan girl, M'pha, considerably grown up since I had last seen her.

I was suddenly aware of the drawn sword still in my hand and blundered into speech. "Deiphobus's blood is on this sword," I heard myself say, and immediately felt a fool. Was that a thing to say to your wife after ten years of separation? It sounded as if I were accusing her. Was I? What were my feelings?

Her hands went to her veil and I felt my muscles tense. After ten years would her beauty still dazzle and confuse me as it always had? Then the veil was gone from her face and I stood speechless. My first reaction was that this woman couldn't be Helen. The fools had confused some other blonde Argive captive with my wife, or perhaps it was some Trojan trick. I almost turned and shouted for my men, but something in that face made me pause for a moment. Then she spoke and it was Helen's voice without any doubt, without any possible doubt.

"Deiphobus didn't matter," she was saying. She took a step toward me and said very seriously with her deep blue eyes—Helen's eyes—fixed on my face, "It was a marriage in form only. You can see why. Aphrodite and I had a falling out," For a moment I didn't understand. Aphrodite? The goddess? What did this woman—did Helen mean by a falling out with Aphrodite? That her beauty had...left her... somehow? Her face...yes, it could be Helen's face with something—the brightness, the glory, the beauty—gone from it, the delicate lines somehow smudged, the lovely proportions subtly altered. What had been a face of beauty surpassing that of any mortal woman was now an ordinary face.

Helen—I was sure now that it was Helen—spoke again. "It did matter when you beat Paris in your single combat with him. If it hadn't been for Aphrodite that would have ended the war then. I wish it had." Confused memories of that fight crowded into my mind: Paris had been at my mercy until some sort of cloud or mist had hidden him from my sight. I had been miserable and confused: all very well to talk of Olympians intervening but I had blamed myself. If I had been a little quicker, a little more resolute. Then what she was saying penetrated my mind. She had wanted me to win, she even sounded proud of me! I felt a kind of warm glow and said impulsively, "Paris didn't matter either. Not if you...."

There was a crash behind me as someone pushed the door open. I wheeled to see my brother, Agamemnon, looking as if he had been doing very little fighting but no doubt prepared as usual to take all the credit for the victory. There have been many times I have not wanted to see my brother thrusting in but this time I wanted him less than I ever had before. He smiled at me cheerfully, unconscious as always that he could possibly be unwelcome. "You all right, youngster?" he asked. "Hot work out there. I heard they'd found Helen, so I came.... Great Zeus, is this her? Lost her looks, has she? Might as well avenge your honor by putting her to the sword, brother, no use showing this to the army as a reason for ten years of fighting."

There was a red haze before my eyes and a roaring in my ears. I raised my sword and if my brother had gone on speaking I think I would have killed him then and there, but Merionathes was saying something to him and somehow this kept me from doing anything. When Agamemnon turned back to me I would cut him down, but I couldn't strike at his back. Now he was turning. . . .

Then there was a voice, perhaps the one voice that could have reached me then, the voice of Odysseus. I hardly took in what he was saying, but as always he was clearing the obstacles from my way; distracting Agamemnon, getting him out of the room.

The tone if not the words of some parting insult of Agamemnon's reached me and I took a step toward him, but Odysseus stepped in front of me and said softly, "I'll keep him out of your way for a while, my friend. Don't hold it too much against him; he is what he is." Then he turned to Aethra and M'pha, getting them out of the room, speaking quietly and respectfully to Helen. "Blessings on both of you," I heard him say, then he and the women were gone and I was alone with Helen.

Her eyes sought mine and there was a question in them. If I answered that question any way but one I would make myself another like Agamemnon. I stepped forward, not sure of my feelings, but sure of what I must do, and took my wife into my arms.

The next morning I woke, not sure for a moment where I was. Solid walls around me instead of a tent, a wide soft bed instead of my cot, a delicate scent in my nostrils ... I looked around at the richly decorated room, then I saw Helen sitting on a low backed chair near the bed. She had a mirror in one hand and was looking into it: there was a comb in her other hand but she was not using it. I rose silently and stood behind her. I saw her face reflected in the bronze mirror and for a moment it was the face I remembered, the face I had dreamed of. I felt a pang of what might have been joy or might have been fear. Then she turned the mirror over and and looked into the silver side, and the face I saw reflected was the face I had seen last night.

"When M'pha's mother first showed me this mirror she told me that when you got to her age you tried to make yourself look as well in the silver side as you looked in the bronze," Helen said quietly. "I'd try to do something to look better, but I've never had to...I don't know how. Perhaps your brother is right, and I should keep my veil on."

A red rage rose in me. "To Hades with Agamemnon," I said harshly. "Go veiled or not as you choose. You're my wife. Agamemnon has nothing to say about it."

She turned and faced me. "I don't mind if they jeer at me," she said, "but I don't want them jeering at you. Perhaps I will go veiled in public for a while. You've been kind, Menelaus, and I thank you for it. I'll make you happy if I can, if you still want me. But if you want to take one of the captive Trojan women as a concubine I won't reproach you. I'll have to remain your wife if you want to keep the throne of Sparta: I wish there wasn't that between us, that... compulsion. I want to go home with you, to be with you. But if, now you've...reclaimed me...you don't want me anymore, I'll understand."

"Who do you think I am? Agamemnon?" I said gruffly. "Of course I won't take a concubine: you're my wife, the mother of my child. Do you think I'd put you to shame like that, even if I. ..."

"Many men would," she said, looking into my eyes. "Perhaps most men. I chose better than I knew when I married you, husband. I've always loved you, but I think I've never respected you enough. Doesn't it...trouble you...that I lived with Paris all these years? It troubled me that you might have put another woman in my place."

"There were women, yes, but none ever took your place," I told her. "Of course it troubled me thinking of you with Paris. But Paris is dead. We're together again. All that is over."

She nodded, a small smile on her lips. "Many things are over, husband. New things are beginning: what will come of them we can only wait and see. Can we . . . will you take me home soon?"

I smiled back at her. "As soon as we can get away," I said, "we'll sail for home. There's not a Danaan here that isn't anxious to get home. I'm lucky enough to have you here, but we'll both be glad to get back to Hermione and to our own place. Away from . . . all this."

She looked at me with that curious little smile. "I suppose I'll have to be content with that for the time being," she said obscurely. "Are you hungry, Menelaus? Lie back down and rest and I'll see what I can find for you in the kitchen." She turned around and went out of the room: I noticed that her walk had all its old grace. I lay back down on the bed feeling curiously frustrated. What did I want from her? Tears? Protestations of innocence? I knew that I would never get either: Helen had lost her beauty, but not her inner strength. Last night she had given me her body, with a passion to match my hungry passion. Today she had spoken of love and respect, even admitted to jealousy. Why then did I feel that she was still not mine?

Was it my fault? Perhaps Helen had expected me to declare my love for her, to tell her that I still loved her, despite the loss of her beauty, despite her years with Paris. Why hadn't I said all that, it was true enough—or was it? While Helen had been the most beautiful woman in the world I had never had any doubt that I loved her devotedly. When Paris stole her away surely the force of my jealousy proved my love. I remembered the nights of agony in my tent on the shore, thinking of her in Paris's arms. Had I really put that jealousy behind me as I had told Helen or did I just not want to think of those times?

No man who really loved a woman would cease to love her because she had lost her beauty. Had I ceased to love Helen? Did that mean that I had never really loved her? Was I more like Agamemnon than I thought, did the loss of Helen's beauty take away my pride in being her husband? If my rulership of Sparta did not depend on my marriage would I put her away and choose another wife? I had thought that I knew myself, but now I was not so sure.

Helen came into the room: if she had waited for me to speak I don't know what I might have said. But she spoke first, her face showing strain and revulsion. "Menelaus, I'm sorry. Our soldiers wouldn't let them disturb us till you woke, but there are urgent messages for you, asking your presence at Council. Ajax the Locrian raped Cassandra in Athena's temple. Now he's claiming sanctuary there. They're debating what to do with him, and Odysseus wants your support."

Chapter Three

THE WOMEN

I'm not sure what impulse made me ask Helen if she would like to accompany me, perhaps only a desire not to be parted from her, as if physical separation would somehow make her less mine. She nodded, a thoughtful look on her face. "Thank you, husband. I think I would like to go with you," she said. "It won't hurt to have a woman there. I don't suppose anyone's given much thought to poor Cassandra; they're all worried about Athena: whether she'd be more offended at having Ajax torn from the sanctuary of her temple to be punished, or at letting him escape unpunished after desecrating that same temple. Odysseus is as likely to guess right as anyone: he knows her well enough...."

I felt the uneasiness that I always felt when the Olympians were mentioned. Life was complicated enough without the interference of powerful immortal beings. I didn't deny their existence, there was plenty of evidence for that, but I preferred not to think about them, or have anything to do with them. Helen, they said, was a daughter of Zeus: I preferred not to think of that either. Along with her fabulous beauty her Olympian blood had always given me a respect for her—no, to be honest, a fear of her. I looked at her as she walked by my side, our little guard of Spartans around us, on our way to the Council. She had lost her beauty but that was not apparent under the veil she now wore. She had not lost, so far as I could see, one bit of her pride or confidence: anyone would have known from her bearing alone that she was a queen.

I had feared some challenge when we entered the Council room which had probably formerly been Priam's throne room, but passions were too high for any extraneous matters to make an impression. Agamemnon was leaning forward on his chair of state, his face flushed, and the speaker's staff was almost being snatched from the previous speaker by the next man eager to speak. Odysseus was leaning back in his chair, apparently calm, but his eyes fastened on me with a sort of urgency as I approached the chair that had been saved for me. There was no chance of getting another chair up to the front of the assembly so I waved Helen to the chair and stood beside her, conspicuous as the only man in the front ranks who was standing.

When Agamemnon saw me he broke in on the man speaking—he was never one to pay much attention to formalities—and addressed me in exasperated tones. "I am glad to see that you have arisen from your bed at last, brother. I have need of your voice," he said. "Some here are saying that we should tear Ajax, son of Oileus, from Athena's sanctuary and punish him...." Out of the comer of my eye I saw Odysseus nod: it was now clear to me which side he was on. Agamemnon continued. "So far as I can see that's bad counsel: what the girl lost can't be restored, and these things happen in the sack of a city. Perhaps it wasn't even in the temple—some fool probably mixed up where it happened and where he fled...."

Odysseus gestured for the speaker's staff with such authority that the man who had snatched it from the previous speaker handed it over, though with a sullen face. Odysseus stood with his head slightly bowed and the staff held with seeming awkwardness in a stiffly outthrust arm, but his marvelous voice seemed to fill the room as he spoke slowly and quietly. "Men of Argos and allies of the High King, I warn you that you are courting destruction. Athena will exact a terrible vengeance for the desecration of her temple. If we punish Ajax ourselves she may spare the rest of us, but if we let the man escape, she will regard us all as equally guilty. After all these weary years we may never reach our homes and wives. Some have said...." Here he darted a glance under his shaggy brows at Agamemnon, "Some have claimed that Athena will be offended if we drag Ajax from her temple where he has barricaded himself, claiming sanctuary! That is as impudent as if a parricide should make a claim for mercy because he was now an orphan! Believe me, Athena is only holding her hand to give us a chance to do our duty and punish the transgressor. What do you say. King Menelaus?"

He walked over and presented the speaker's staff to me with a courteous gesture and a little smile. My heart pounded and my head seemed filled with wool. Of course I would support my friend against Agamemnon; aside from anything else in any disagreement between the two, Odysseus was sure to be right. But how best to do it? Open opposition would only infuriate my brother: in fact, his present headstrong attitude was probably due to jealousy of Odysseus whose stratagem with the Horse had finally gained us entry into Troy. On the rare occasions when Odysseus couldn't manage my brother it was because he overestimated Agamamnon, forgot how childish and unreasonable he could be. I was not likely to forget that, and for once I might manage him when Odysseus had failed. First I must smooth him down....

"My brother is wise to delay a decision until all the facts are known certainly," I said, trying to keep any irony out of my voice. "Once we are sure that Cassandra was violated in the sanctuary itself our course of action will be clear: we dare not offend the Olympians by condoning the desecration of a temple. Are there witnesses who can swear to what happened?"

Agamemnon's nostrils flared and his face darkened, but I had been tactful enough to avoid an immediate outburst. "All right," he growled ungraciously, "bring in the girl herself. Let her make her complaint." I felt Helen stir in her chair beside me and I realized why: it was barbarous to drag the girl into this assembly and make her tell the story of her rape. But a protest now would only enrage Agamemnon and cause him to do something even more outrageous. Perhaps Cassandra's ordeal would ensure the punishment of her attacker, at least. Anyway, some of the guards had already gone to get the girl: it was too late to protest.

Was there anything else I could say while I had the speaker's staff? Agamemnon solved that problem for me temporarily by grumbling on in a querulous tone, "I don't know why there's all this fuss about one Trojan girl. We don't want disunity in our ranks now in the moment of victory...." Suddenly much became clear to me. Agamemnon cared nothing for Ajax, but he hoped to keep in peacetime the dominance over his allies that he had maintained during these years of war. He was balking at punishing Ajax because he didn't want to antagonize the Locrians. Agamemnon grumbled on, steadily ignoring the fact that it was the desecration of the temple that was at issue, and the danger to all of us from an outraged Olympian.

"What in Hades' Halls...?" said Agamemnon as weeping and wailing came from the corridor outside. There was certainly more than one woman out there. Harassed-looking guards came in with a little group of women in stained and rumpled garments that still showed evidence of their high rank: they even retained a few ornaments that had not been snatched away by greedy fingers. All of them except one girl were weeping and moaning, and about her quiet there was an air of strain, almost of desperation. Somehow I was sure that this was Cassandra, but the guard said apologetically, "None of them speak Danaan, and they all kept carrying on like this. When I asked for Cassandra they just wailed the more. All I could do was bring all of them, King Agamemnon."

Suddenly one of the women broke off her weeping and took a step toward Agamemnon, her face so contorted with fury that for an instant he quailed back in fear. "I speak your filthy language,'" she cried, "but I wouldn't soil my tongue with it, except to curse you, Agamemnon, 'King of men.' I am Andromache, wife of Hector, the bravest and noblest of your enemies. I do not curse you because Achilles killed my husband: that was in fair fight. I do not curse you because you Argives sacked my city and took me captive: such is war. But because your Argives tore from my arms my child, my little Astynax, Hector's only son and threw him from the walls of Troy to his death, I curse you and all your people. May your homecoming be bitter, may your own children die as mine has died, may your wives weep as I weep...."

My hand was on Helen's shoulder: I could feel her shudder as Andromache spoke of the child's death. I was sick myself at the thought of it. It is hardly ever the real fighters who do that sort of thing, taking out their frustrations on the helpless; it is the jackals like Thersites who would have run like the wind from Hector living, who would take "vengeance" on him by snatching his child from his wife's arms and killing it. Thersites was dead: it could not have been him, but whoever did it would no doubt be boasting of his deed.

"Lady," I said impulsively, "whoever killed Hector's son in that fashion dishonored our victory. If he can be found he'll answer to me." Andromache seemed to shrivel: without opposition to keep up her fury her sorrow overwhelmed her. She gave me no answer except to weep and speak her child's name over and over as the guards led her out. Most of the remaining women were obviously too old to be Cassandra and I was still sure that she must be the silent one. Suddenly a thought struck me and I spoke again.

"My wife knows Cassandra and speaks the Trojan tongue," I said. "Let her question the girl." Helen rose to her feet, not waiting for Agamemnon to speak, and said in a commanding voice, "Cassandra!" There was a murmur among the Argive leaders and for a moment I thought that someone would raise a protest. But then I heard Odysseus's deep tones saying, "Silence for the Queen of Sparta," and the murmurs ceased. They were used to listening to that voice in moments of crisis.

Helen spoke again, a flood of half-familiar syllables. I speak enough Cretan to get by and many of the Trojan words are the same or similar. I noticed, as I had not consciously noticed before, how beautiful Helen's voice still was, a voice of gold with grace in every lilting note. Before she had finished speaking every eye in the room was on that veiled figure.

Even Cassandra seemed to relax a little. When she began to answer Helen her voice was low and hesitant but it grew a little louder and more confident. I recognized a word that was the same in Cretan, repeated several times, "Asos," "the holy place," "the temple." Helen turned to Agamemnon and said quietly, "King Agamemnon, Cassandra confirms that Ajax raped her in the temple itself: he tore her away from the statue of Athena she was clinging to and it toppled over. Something must have weakened the base." She looked at Odysseus as she said this and he gave a little smile. The wooden figure he had stolen from Troy had been hidden in the base of that statue.

Agamemnon did not reply; he was staring at Cassandra. "Ask her if she went to the Sowing Festival three years ago," he said in a strange voice. For Agamemnon the request was a polite one. Helen bowed her head in assent and spoke to Cassandra again. When she spoke to Agamemnon again there was a delicate irony in her voice that was lost on Agamemnon but not on Odysseus or on me.

"She says, King Agamemnon, that she was indeed at the Sowing Festival in honor of the Great Mother and that there her prophetic gift led her to submit to the Sacred Mating with an Argive Lord. She bore twin sons to that Argive and has hidden them safely during the sack of the City."

Agamemnon's demeanor made it obvious to me just who that Argive Lord had been. "Two sons," he murmured with a complacaent smile. "Two sons and both safe." Then a thought struck him and his face grew dark again. He turned to the captain of the guards and snapped, "Take a force large enough to do the job and get Ajax out of that temple. Bring him before me."

There was renewed murmuring in the hall as Agamemnon sank back in his chair, still gazing at Cassandra. My eyes met those of Odysseus across the room and he shook his head incredulously. What a turn of events! But at least this meant that Ajax would be punished and Athena's wrath perhaps averted from us. Helen turned to me and spoke in a voice that was clear, but so low that only I could hear it, a trick of hers that I had half forgotten. "I hope no one else here speaks enough of the tongue of Ilium to know what else Cassandra said," Helen murmured. "She said that her prophetic gift tells her that every man who lies with her will die: Ajax first and Agamemnon before the year is out."

My eyes flew to my brother and I looked at him with a sort of horrified fascination. Surely the prophecy was nonsense, yet... dead before the year was out, the girl had said. Somehow, I realized, I had never thought of Agamemnon as mortal: I had thought I would have him on my neck forever.

Agamemnon pulled himself up in a way I knew: it meant that he had reached a decision, probably a foolish one. Suddenly I felt almost fond of him. In the light of that prophecy even his faults seemed for the moment endearing. He rose to his feet, and Helen sank into her chair with a graceful movement as if giving him the right to speak.

"I claim this girl, Princess Cassandra, daughter of Priam, as part of my share of the spoils of Troy," said Agamemnon. "The other women of the royal family I will bestow on our greatest warriors to do with as they will. Odysseus, Queen Hecuba falls to your share, as is due to our greatest warrior. Neoptolomos, son of Achilles, I give you Andromache, Hector's wife." Typical Agamemnon decisions both: he was probably trying to insult Odysseus by giving him the aged Queen and revenge himself on Andromache for her outburst by giving her to the son of the man who had killed her husband. "As for Ajax..." he began. But he was interrupted by one of the guards who had been sent for Ajax who burst into the room with blood on his face and tears in his eyes. "My lord Agamemnon," he gasped, "Ajax burst out of the Temple and cut through us: by now he must be halfway to his ship!"

Chapter Four

ENDINGS

I turned and ran from the room, seeing from the corner of my eye that Odysseus was close behind me. Diomedes, of course was on his heels, but it was not until we were outside that I realized that Helen had followed us out. "I know the City," she said laconically. "Find us a chariot and I'll be your driver." Diomedes and Odysseus were shouting for their teams and their men were bringing them up. I realized that my own chariot and horses might still be at the ships. Helen stepped forward and said to Diomedes, "Those are the horses you got from Aeneus, aren't they? Let Menelaus and I take that chariot and you go with Odysseus. Follow our chariot and I'll get you out of the City the quickest way."

Diomedes glanced over at Odysseus, who nodded. The big man handed Helen into the chariot with a bow and a grin and she had the horses moving almost before I had scrambled in. Odysseus let us pass him and then followed us a short spear-cast behind, Diomedes riding beside him with his arms folded, taking the jolts and the swerves with a grace that made it seem easy. I was holding hard to the rail of our chariot: not having a spear and shield to hold I saw no point in showing off by not holding on. Helen handled the reins as well as any charioteer I had ever seen. She had learned some of these unfeminine skills from Theseus during her captivity in Attika, and had always driven her own chariot in Sparta, but I wondered how she had kept in practice in the beleaguered city.

We rattled and crashed down the streets of Troy, skillfully avoiding the occasional body in the streets and the even more occasional man on foot. "Most of them will be looters," I told Helen. "Don't go to too much trouble to avoid running them down." She nodded but said nothing: she had thrown back her veil to see better and her eyes were narrowed with concentration as she steered the heavy war chariot through the narrow streets.

Presently we were out of the streets and into the little courtyard in front of the Scaean Gate. The Horse still stood there, stark against the morning sky and Helen gave me a little grin as we passed it. There was a little picket of Argive troops before the gate and she pulled the chariot up while I shouted, "Has Ajax the Locrian been through here?"

The man in charge of the guards was, luckily, intelligent and alert: he was already gesturing for his men to clear the barricade before the damaged gate as he yelled back, "No, King Menelaus, but one of my men spotted a man coming over the wall on a rope just a few minutes ago. I sent men to chase him but he got away. A looter, we thought. Anyway, an Argive."

"Good man," I said. "Keep the barrier open, there'll be others behind us." Then we were off again, just as Odysseus and Diomedes caught us up. They didn't even have to check their pace as they stormed through the gate. As we emerged onto the flat plain they drew abreast of us for a moment, with Diomedes urging Odysseus on, but soon the lighter weight in our chariot and the quality of Aeneus's horses enabled us to draw ahead again. I looked behind us and saw Odysseus shake his head as Diomedes urged him to whip up the horses: the wily Ithakan was not about to risk his horses or his neck going at the speed his companion wanted.

Helen snatched her veil from her shoulders just as it was about to blow away and handed it to me with one hand while she handled the reins with the other. Seeing that her garment was billowing in the wind I braced myself against the motion of the chariot and used both hands to tie the veil around her waist as a sash. She gave me a smile, then turned her eyes back to the ground ahead of us. With her hair loosened and blowing behind her and her cheeks rosy from the wind whipping in her face, she seemed for the moment to have a new kind of beauty: I had a feeling that I was getting a glimpse of the girl who had hunted and ridden with Theseus.

Before long we were at the shore: I headed for one end of the line of ships, for I knew that the ship of Odysseus would be in this post of honor and danger and that he would have left a crew with his ship. No telling where Agamemnon had told them to beach my ship and I had no time to find out. The Ithakan captain saluted when he recognized me and said, "A Locrian ship just launched, King Menelaus. I didn't know what it was about, but I got our ship ready just in case."

"Good man," I said. Any man Odysseus left in charge of his ship would be that, though. "Get her in the water," I told him. "We'll follow the Locrians as soon as King Odysseus gets here." I leant a shoulder to get the black ship down the rollers while Helen unhitched the horses with deft fingers and tethered them to a tent peg someone had left driven into the rocky shore.

Almost as soon as the ship was afloat Odysseus and Diomedes pulled up on the beach in a shower of sand and pebbles and ran for the ship. Diomedes grinned at Helen and roared,. "By the gods, you can drive a team, Lady. If you get tired of redhead here, come to Argos and be my queen!"

Helen smiled and said, "I'm not much use pulling an oar, though. Leave your team with me and get after that

Locrian ship." Diomedes saluted her, splashed into the water and pulled himself up over the side of the ship with one heave of his mighty muscles. Odysseus and I scrambled up the side in a more conventional fashion, helped by the men aboard, and he went to the steering oar while I took the oar opposite Diomedes, hoping I could keep up with his stroke.

"Ready! Give way!" came the deep voice of Odysseus and the sea-roving Ithakan's black ship sprang from the shore like a dog on the tail of a fox.

For a few moments I was conscious of nothing but the frantic labor of rowing, while the throbbing of some bumps and cuts reminded me of fighting yesterday and tired legs reminded one of how I had spent some of the night. Then Odysseus's voice came again. "Rest on your oars." I saw him take his hand from the steering oar and reach down to the deck beside him. He came up with one of his massive bows that few men besides himself could even draw. He strung the bow with one easy motion of powerful arms and shoulders, then reached down again and rummaged in some sort of container attached to the side of the ship. He produced a long black arrow, wickedly barbed, nocked the arrow and began to draw the bow. I looked over my shoulder to see what his target was.

The Locrian ship was a long bowshot ahead of us, but I could see the steersman clearly enough, and if Odysseus could see him he could probably put an arrow through him. In the confusion we could put on a spurt, catch the Locrian ship and board her.

But then, out of the clear blue skies lightning leaped down and struck the Locrian ship, not just one bolt but three, one after the other! Even the seasoned sea-rovers of Odysseus's crew were pale and trembling as the peals of thunder sounded in our ears, and I could hear Diomedes cursing, or maybe praying, under his breath in the silence that followed the peals.

"The gray-eyed Lady took her own vengeance," said Odysseus and even his deep, quiet voice was touched with awe. There was not a sign of the ship: it had been blasted to pieces and scattered like a heap of straw caught in a hard gust of wind. Then a sailor shouted, "There's someone swimming!" and Diomedes exclaimed, "By the God, it's Ajax! The tough little bastard is swimming away!" There was a reluctant admiration in his tone, but Odysseus was already nocking his arrow again as the swimmer headed for a little rocky islet that was the last outcrop of the jagged promontory which sheltered the landing beach.

Ajax reached the islet, pulled himself up and shook a fist at the sky, shouting something we could not hear. Odysseus was raising his bow again when the little island heaved and shook, seeming to break into pieces. Ajax fell shrieking into a chasm that opened at his feet and rocks cascaded down on him. We could hear his cries for what seemed a long time, before the water rushed into the crevice and the cries ended in a horrible gurgle. Diomedes shook himself like a big dog and muttered, "Grant that she's never angry at me!" I didn't need to ask who "she" was: Ajax had paid horribly for his desecration of Athena's temple.

The ship gave a sudden heave and my guts were cold with fear, but it was only a stiff wind that had come up to whip the waves into white-caps and make the ship pitch and roll. For a moment I relaxed, then I heard Odysseus say quietly but urgently, "Back to shore, quick and draw her well up. The wrath of Athena is over the sea and we'll be lucky if she leaves us our ships to go home on: luckier still if she doesn't sink us when we do try to get home."

We made it to shore, though I wonder if we would have if two of Athena's favorites had not been on board. When we reached shore Helen, veiled again, was already organizing the men left to guard the ships to draw them up as high on the shore as possible. Wind whipped rollers were already dashing on the sterns of the ships and the waves seemed to suck hungrily at the ships when they receded, as if to draw them out to sea.

We got the lighter ships up the beach first, and by the time we got to the bigger, heavier ships Helen had contrived a harness that would let the chariot horses help in moving the bigger ships. It was heavy work for a while but presently all the ships were too high on the shore to be affected by even the biggest breakers, and Helen was handing round skins of wine and whatever emergency food she could find in the ships. I noticed that the men treated her with awe, saluting her more as they would a goddess than as they would a mortal queen.

When I saw that Helen was hitching the horses back to the chariots while we ate, I finished my meal hastily and went to help her. She had tied her veil across her face in a way that left her eyes visible, and though I could not see her lips, I could see the smile in her eyes as she glanced up at me. Before we quite had the teams hitched Diomedes and Odysseus had finished at the ships and walked over to join us.

Helen looked over at Odysseus and asked, "How long will Athena close the seas to us?"

He shook his head and said soberly, "No way of knowing, my Lady: it may be more of a warning than an attempt to keep us here at Troy. For my part I'll launch my ship as soon as these seas moderate, for it's no use hiding from an Olympian's wrath. Might as well face it out as you've done. I mean...." For once I saw Odysseus embarrassed at choosing the wrong words, but Helen gave a little chuckle.

"I know what you mean, Odysseus," she said. "And you're quite right. I let Aphrodite bully me into going with Paris, and into staying with him rather than trying to escape from Troy. But when she wanted to send me off with Aeneus just as the war was ending I defied her, and the world didn't come to an end." I must have made some movement because she turned to me and I could see the smile in her eyes again.

"No, I hadn't told you all that, had I, Menelaus?" she said. "Perhaps I should have. I know that there are times when my pride keeps me from telling you things which would sound like excusing myself. Aphrodite didn't kill me and I don't think Athena will either. I want to get home to Sparta and Hermione as soon as possible: can we launch our ships when Odysseus and Diomedes launch theirs?"

"Of course," I told her, trying to speak matter-of-factly to hide my emotions. "Agamemnon won't like it but so much the worse for him. They're probably still arguing in Council: let's get back and tell them we're going." It would have been easier to simply go, without getting into an argument with my brother, but I was not going to sneak off like a runaway servant. For once, I would face Agamemnon down.

My brother was just as angry as I thought he would be: he was clinging desperately to his fading authority as commander in chief, and that would be gone as soon as the expeditionary force broke up into separate contingents to return home. "Don't be a fool, Menelaus," he blustered.

"The sensible thing is to stay here a while longer and wait until the wrath of the gods cools. We can make sacrifices to try to appease the Olympians...."

I stood up and looked him in the eyes, my anger kindled by the memories those words brought back. "As you sacrificed your daughter when the winds were against us ten years ago?" I asked bitingly.

He was taken aback, but tried to bluster it out. "They say only blood will satisfy the wrath of the gods," he said. "We could sacrifice one of Priam's daughters at the tomb of Achilles...."

The glitter in his eyes as he said this was the last straw. "I'm sick of killing, Agamemnon," I told him. "And I'm sick of taking orders from you. Give over killing and go home to your wife and children. I'm taking my wife and my Spartans and launching my ships as soon as the wind dies down." As I shouldered my way from the room I heard first Odysseus and then Diomedes tell Agamemnon that they too were leaving, and some of the others simply began to leave the Council without bothering to declare their intention of leaving.

I had done it at last, stood up to my brother and defied him. And as Helen had said of her confrontation with Aphrodite, the heavens had not fallen. I wished Agamemnon no evil, so long as he left me alone, but I resolved to keep him at a distance from now on. He had always assumed that his son Orestes would marry my Hermione, but I'd have none of that. Odysseus's boy, Telemachus, was too old for Hermione, might even be married by the time we reached home, but there were plenty of fine young men who would be happy enough to marry the heiress of Sparta, despite the wrath of Agamemnon. Perhaps young Neoptolemos would be a good choice: he had some of his father's virtues without his bad points. And Agamemnon would think twice about arguing with the son of Achilles!

I chuckled at the thought and Helen looked at me inquiringly. "What do you think of Neoptolemos for Hermione?" I asked.

She laughed and said, "Plenty of time to think of husbands for her, Menelaus. She's only a child. How wonderful to think I'll soon see her again...."

But when we reached the shore and launched our ships in a deceptive lull in the storm, we soon found ourselves tossing among monstrous waves, being blown farther and farther off course, farther from home and Hermione.

Chapter Five

THE ISLAND OF THE SEALS

I soon saw that there was nothing to do but run before the storm, hoping to rendezvous with our other ships when the wind died down. As soon as we stopped fighting the wind the motion of the ship eased, and if it were not for the thought of our daughter and our kingdom, I would have been happy enough with Helen by my side and free at last of the sullen shore where we had warred for so long. The world was wide: I had a crew of the best fighting men in the world and a golden ballast in the hold.

But it was the treasure we carried which worried me when my shipmaster told me that the winds were carrying us toward Egypt. I shared my worries with Helen soon after he gave me the news. "The Pharoahs are a law to themselves," I said. "The fact that we're the King and Queen of Sparta will impress the Egyptians very little, and if Pharoah's officials decide to take a look at our cargo there's very little we could do about it. Sparta isn't enough of a sea power to do much in retaliation, even if they let us escape with our lives."

Helen frowned thoughtfully and said, "If we do land we'll have to pretend to be traders and begin by sending gifts to Pharoah as the traders do. It will give us a certain protected status and the 'gifts' Pharoah sends in return will be as close in value to our 'gifts' as most merchants would give in a fair trade. I know all this from M'pha: her family are sea traders and she's often told me stories about trading. But it's true that some Egyptian officials are corrupt, according to those same stories. It might be safest not to land at an Egyptian port at all if we can avoid it. Ask your shipmaster if there's any chance of waiting out these winds in an uninhabitcd place or at least some village too small to have much of a garrison."

The shipmaster was a grizzled Cretan who like many Cretans made his livelihood by sailing ships for less sea-wise countries. He was respectful but dubious.

"It's true enough that you'll do well to avoid Egyptian officials if you can," he said, "and the Lady is right to say that if we must go into an Egyptian port we should go in as traders. They won't believe us, of course. Any ship with this many armed men will be suspected of being a raider. But if we go through the proper motions they'll think twice about boarding us or seizing our cargo: Egyptians depend on trade for a good many luxuries, and they don't want to discourage traders. If we must go into a port it had better be a big one; at any small port they'd think we were looking the place over as if to sack the town, and they'd send for troops as soon as they saw us. The coasts are too well watched for a landing in some uninhabited place...."

He pulled thoughtfully at his chin whiskers and then said slowly, "There's one place that might do: a little island about a day's good sail from the mouth of the Nile. Traders sometimes stop there to shift cargo when the first day's sailing shows problems with the way it's been stowed. There's water there, but nothing to eat except fish. We couldn't stay there forever, but if we can make it at all with these winds we might be able to wait out a shift in the winds there."

It seemed the best solution of those that were offered, and I told him to make a landing on the island if he could. We were very nearly blown right past it, but by striking the sail and laboring at the oars for weary hours, we were able to first get into the lee of the island and eventually land on it.

It was a barren place, little more than sand and rock, with little alive on it but seabirds and a large herd of seals, but it had a sheltered cove and we were glad enough to ground our keel on the shingle and stretch our weary legs. My shipmaster drew me aside and said earnestly, "King Menelaus, you spoke words of praise for my skill when we sighted this island; trust me now. Order your men to leave those seals strictly alone—by no means to harm or torment them. They say that these seals are under the protection of the People Under the Sea and that any sailor who harms one of them is dooming his shipmates to a grave in the sea, for the Undersea Folk will sink his ship in revenge. Perhaps it is just a tale, my Lord, but it is not one I care to test."

I gave the order, as much for the sake of the animals as because of the shipmaster's tale: if I had not the men would very likely have hunted them or used them for target practice, merely out of boredom. Whatever else you can say about Spartans, they are well-disciplined, and my orders were obeyed. But as the weary days went by with no change in the wind I grew curious about the seals myself and spent much of my time watching them. As they grew used to me they let me approach the herd closer and closer, until I was actually able to walk among the herd without causing them to slip back into the sea.

Helen had been swimming a good deal and sunning herself in the hot southern sunlight while I restlessly wandered the barren island. When I told her one night of my success with the seals she smiled and said, "You're always surprising me, Menelaus. I'd like to see these pets of yours if I may. I don't think I'll frighten them: animals generally like me." She took a few sensible precautions when we set off the next morning, wearing a dark garment and a dark cloth over her hair, which was still golden though it seemed to have lost some of its luster.

As we walked toward the beach I told her the shipmaster's story and she took it a good deal more seriously than I had. "I know you're a bit wary of the Olympians and anything to do with them, Menelaus," she said, "and I don't ordinarily trouble you with things I know or feel that are... out of the ordinary. But some kind of Wild People are around this island. I've known that ever since we got here. This far out at sea, on an island this barren they can only be Those Under the Sea, and they're wildest of the wild. If the seals are under their protection they probably won't be far away, so don't be surprised if you see something... unusual."

If I could have done it without seeming a fool in my own eyes I would have turned back at that: Helen would never have reproached me. But I would have reproached myself, and so I went on, feeling a good deal less happy about our expedition. When we got to the seals, though, I forgot my worries for a while. When you got used to their strange appearance—and their smell!—they were rather beautiful animals. The young ones were especially delightful, reminding me of puppies in my kennels at home. I had brought a few hounds to the war with me but no bitches and seeing the hard life for animals in our camp on the beach at Troy I had not sent for any. So it was a long time since I had played with a young animal and the young seals were frisky little things with an alert, intelligent look.

I was trying to coax one to come closer to me, when suddenly I realized that Helen and I were not alone. I glanced up to see a young woman so ordinary looking at first glance my first thought was that another ship must have landed on the island and she was a passenger stretching her legs. Then I saw the slightly slanted, sea-green eyes with a look in them that made me catch my breath. Suddenly I realized why they

called the nymphs the Wild Girls: those eyes were as alien
from humankind as the liquid eyes of the seal pup she held
in her arms. She handed it to me with a little half smile and
I took the young animal from her and petted it as if in a
dream.

The Wild Girl stooped and picked up the seal pup I
had been coaxing and gave it to Helen who accepted it with
a smile, and said in the low soothing voice she had used to
calm the horses on the beach of Troy: "I am Helen and this
is Menelaus. We come in peace."

The Wild Girl looked at us for a moment and then
said in a voice as strange and remote from humankind as her
eyes, "I am Eidothee." She looked at us without speaking
for a while as the seal pup wriggled in my arms, then said to
Helen, "He's quite pretty. Is he yours?" At Helen's smiling
nod the sea-nymph gave a delicate little shrug and said. "Oh
well... there will be others. You're one of the Shining people,
aren't you? Except not quite...."

Helen smiled a little sadly and said, "My mother was
mortal, but Zeus is my father...." Somehow the little bow of
reverence that the Wild Girl gave at that name brought home
Helen's Olympian heritage as nothing else had ever done. I
wondered suddenly how much of that side of herself Helen
had kept hidden from me just because she knew my uneasy
feelings about it.

The sea-girl turned her eyes on me again and said
musingly, "We don't like mortals here too long, usually, but
I suppose...." Helen spoke in the little pause that followed,
spoke quietly, but persuasively, her golden voice almost
cajoling, "Eidothee, we'd be happy to leave your island,
but the winds won't let us sail to our home. They're not
natural winds; do the People of the Sea know anything about

them?"

Eidothee gave another little shrug, her face indifferent. "I wouldn't know," she said. Then a little mischievous glint came into her eyes. "Father would know," she said, "and if you could hold on to him he'd have to tell you. That wouldn't be easy, though, he's a shape-changer, not just animals but things like fire and ice.... Why don't you try? I'd like to watch...."

Helen's eyes met mine and I knew that she knew the fear in my heart, a fear I had never felt in the press of battle. She said nothing, but somehow I drew strength from that gaze, strength to turn to the Wild Girl and ask, "How can I find him?" She gave a little trill of laughter that made her seem less human: somehow I could imagine that same chiming laughter sounding as a ship which sheltered a man who had offended her folk sank beneath the waves.

"Oh, he'll soon be here to inspect the flock," she said. "I'm first here because I like to swim ahead. Lie down in that hollow and I'll call the flock around you." At first I didn't realize what she meant by the "flock," but as I saw the seals begin to shuffle toward us on their flippers I realized that they were the flock she meant. Taking a deep breath I lay myself down in the little sandy hollow she had pointed out, and felt Helen's soft body close to mine as she lay down beside me. The Wild Girl nudged and prodded her "flock" until we were totally concealed by tails and flippers. One of the seal pups wriggled onto my shoulders and I could smell his fishy breath even over the combined odor of the other sea creatures.

I heard the sea nymph's voice above us. "His name is Proteus," she said. "Sometimes it helps to know that."

Then I could sense that she was gone. "Proteus—the

Old Man of the Sea," I whispered to Helen, a dozen half-forgotten tales and stories filling my thoughts.

"Yes," she whispered, "but better be quiet; they have keen ears." I wasn't sure whether "they" were the seals or Proteus and his court of sea nymphs, and I didn't dare speak further to ask.

A dozen times I was sure that one of the great sea-beasts would slither over and crush us, but whatever binding the sea-girl had laid on them held, and despite a few moments that made my heart seem to stop they held the positions the nymph had put them in, concealing us but not crushing us. For a while they shifted restlessly, then a stillness fell on them, and I could feel a Presence pass among them. Only Helen's body pressed to mine kept me from leaping up to flee or fight, so powerful was the feeling that something wild and powerful was within a few paces of us.

Presently I grew almost used to that feeling. Whatever had caused it had not gone away, but the pressure on my nerves gradually grew tolerable. Cautiously, ever so cautiously, I raised my head to look. Drowsing against a rock was a male figure, bearded and with long hair. He was naked and his rotundity would have seemed comic if it were not so obvious that under those rounded contours were muscles to match those of the great sea creatures around us.

No use waiting, no use reflecting that those massive arms could bat me aside as easily as I could swat a fly. I launched myself at the sleeping giant, grasping frantically at the tangled hair and beard. The blow or the crushing bear hug I had expected did not come: instead there was a strange shifting in the form I grasped. There was a roaring in my ears and my fingers were locked into the mane of a great lion!

Whether this was illusion or a real change I felt a sick

certainty that if those teeth reached my throat I would die. I flung myself on the creature's back, still grasping its mane, and tried to lock my legs around its waist. The waist was slim... too slim: I was bestriding a monstrous serpent, my fingers still locked in some sort of growth, more tentacles than hair, at its head. Boneless undulations nearly threw me off, but I clung desperately and tried to grasp tighter with my elbows on either side of it.

My elbows were forced apart as the form expanded to that of a great panther, what my fingers seemed to hold now were handfuls of furry skin that tried to writhe out from my frantic hold. Then I held the bristly skin of a giant boar: I could hear the shuffling grunts as it tried to buck me off. Up it reared, up, up, and now I was trying to grasp a great tree, my fingers locked into the leaves near its crown and the ground far below.

Suddenly there seemed only a great column of water in my grasp: I almost let go my hold then, but there was something solid, the gods knew what, under my fingers and I clung frantically to that. Icier and icier the water grew till my fingers, my legs, my belly all seemed turned to ice. Then a blast of searing heat, and I seemed to grasp a fiery pillar ascending to the sky. I shut my eyes against the glare and held on, held on. Then there was hair again between my fingers and smooth skin where my arms and legs grasped, and I was neither frozen nor burned, but more tired than I had ever been in my life. A deep voice rumbled in my ear, "Well, well, little earthwalker, you have won fairly: loose your hold and the Old Man of the Sea will answer your questions."

Chapter Six

THE PROPHECY OF PROTEUS

"Will you swear by the River of Death, Proteus?" I gasped out. The creature I held chuckled deeply and swore; only then did I loose my hold.

"Well held, earthwalker," he rumbled. "If you hold on to all that is worth holding on to that well you'll be blessed." His strange sea-green eyes flicked over to Helen and he gave her a little salute. "Hail, daughter of the King Above," he said. "I hope that your man is as wise as he is stubborn."

Helen gave a graceful shrug. "No mortal has your wisdom, Proteus," she said. "That's why Menelaus laid hold of you, to learn how we can win back to our home and our child."

The strangeness of my experience had almost put this out of my mind, but at this hint from my wife I turned to Proteus and said, "Tell us, Old Man of the Sea, how we can get home, and what we will find there."

The sea-god turned his face to me and looked at me without expression for a moment, then said in his deep voice with an echo of the sea in it, "You're either lucky or wise, Menelaus, perhaps a little of both. Yes, I'll tell you what you'll find when you reach home, for good or ill. You'll find your brother's been killed by his wife and her lover, and the two of them so well entrenched in Mykenae as to make any attempt at vengeance impossible. Leave them to the vengeance the Olympians will prepare for them. As for your daughter, don't fret about her. She has beauty, but not the fatal beauty that embroiled her mother in kidnapping and war. She is like her father, she holds on to things; and she has not forgotten either of you."

Proteus paused, then went on more slowly. "She will have to hold on a little longer, for the Olympians do not mean to let any of the Argives win home too safely or too easily. As for you, Menelaus, you can only get home by sailing away from it: the Olympians have something waiting for you in Egypt, something that even I may not tell you of. Let the winds take you up the Nile, anchor at the first port you come to and accept what the gods have waiting for you there. The choice you make will determine what your future will be,"

It seemed little enough in the way of information for the struggle I had been through, but at least it told me that it was no use waiting here on the island: we might as well sail for Egypt and see what fate the gods had in store for us. It was good to know that Hermione was well and that she remembered us—ten years is a long time in the life of a young girl. I turned to Helen. "Is there anything you wish to ask him?" I said to her.

She smiled and shook her head, "Probably not, even if he'd answer. But he wouldn't: it was you that caught and held him and it is only your questions he is bound to answer, not mine, even if mine are transmitted through you. Am I right, Proteus?" The Old Man of the Sea chuckled again. "A bargain is a bargain," he said. "It was your questions I said I'd answer, and I've told you what you need to know. Be content, Menelaus; what else I could tell you would only trouble you, until the event teaches you its meaning in its own hour."

Perhaps I should have left it at that, but there was one question I thought that Helen might like the answer to. "One more question and then we'll leave you and your flock in peace, Proteus," I said. "This is my question, for I know that my wife would never ask it. Will Helen ever recover her beauty?"

The sea god looked at me a long moment and then smiled, a smile that I could not read. "Why Helen has never lost her beauty, Menelaus," he said. Then he made some signal to his "flock" and the seals began slipping into the sea one after the other. I looked away from him for a moment to observe the curious change from their clumsy waddle on land to their graceful movements in the water. When I turned back the Old Man of the Sea too was gone.

I turned to Helen and the expression on her face was as unreadable as the smile of Proteus. "Well," I said awkwardly, "we might as well get the men together for the voyage up the Nile. If we have to go, we might as well go at once, and hope the voyage brings us what we want."

Helen smiled, but it seemed to me that her smile was touched with sadness. "Yes, Menelaus," she said softly, "Let us hope that both of us get what we want."

I suppose that every Danaan feels a little like a child in the great cities of Egypt: the kingdom of Pharoah is so vast and so ancient. Even the kingdom of the Sea-King of Crete is young compared to Egypt, and the lands watered by the Nile and ruled by Pharoah are broader and richer than all the Danaan lands. The little dark men with shaven heads in their linen kilts are not impressive, but there were so many of them, porters and servants, merchants and scribes, royal officials and priests of old, dark gods. There is a foolish old tale that the Myrmidons are ants made into men, but if any race of men were transformed ants it seemed to me that it would be these dark, busy, little men of Egypt.

There was a good deal of foreign shipping in the port, for Egyptians are not great sailors and let the sea trade come to them. We were able to drop our anchor stone and moor in a clear spot that had probably been left by a departing ship, without arousing a great deal of attention. Presently a boat came out from the shore to meet us; almost certainly from the harbor master. I heaved a sigh of relief when the fat, self-important official came aboard, gave a cursory look around him and let himself be ushered to a seat and plied with wine and what food we could produce for him. It was very different from landing in Amnisos or Pheastos on Crete, where the Sea King's officials were keen eyed and knowledgeable: most of them former sea captains tired of long voyaging away from home and family.

We had treasure to spare; it was easy enough to find rich gifts for Pharoah and satisfactory bribes to keep the port official happy. Indeed, the problem was rather to find gifts which were not too rich, for we had in our hold the spoil of one of the richest cities in any land. I didn't myself know half of what we had: there were men in my following who were charged with seeing that I got my share of what was being divided. In addition, bales of stuff had come from the House of the Golden Lintel under Helen's direction: her inheritance from Paris no doubt, though I preferred not to think of that. Some of it would be gifts given to her. In the days of her beauty men would give her rich gifts just for the pleasure of seeing her smile.

At last the official stood up to go. Besides being grossly fat, he had a high, fluting voice and I wondered if he was a eunuch. "Your tribute will be conveyed to Pharoah, captain," he piped, "but the Lord of the Two Lands has weighty responsibilities and rarely receives representatives of the People of the Sea in person any longer. In due course you will receive some signs of Pharoah's gracious favor, and after that you may carry on whatever trade you will with the merchants ashore. Many merchants will be very anxious to entertain you while you are waiting to receive the Pharoah's bounty, in hopes that you will choose to trade with them rather than their rivals, but they know the rules and until you hear from Pharoah they will not speak of trade. Enjoy their hospitality, captain; it commits you to nothing." He tittered, heaved his great bulk over the side and was rowed back to shore, I suspected that this perfunctory visit was his work for the day and that he was returning to a rest he no doubt felt was well earned.

The prohibition against trade until Pharoah had acknowledged our gifts evidently did not apply to the provision boats which plied the harbor; they were soon clustered around us offering fresh fruits and delicacies of every kind. Our quartermaster, I was pleased to see, consulted with Helen before making his purchases; she was quietly stepping into her place as mistress of my household.

As soon as the provision boats left us, a procession of richly decorated barges began; wealthy merchants or their representatives, pressing on us invitations to attend banquets, to become houseguests, to join in various expeditions of pleasure or attend a variety of entertainments. I turned all of the invitations aside on the excuse that we were weary from our voyage. I had no idea what the Olympians wanted us here in Egypt for, but I doubted if it was to feast and entertain ourselves.

Presently there came a barge unlike any of the others; the rich odors that wafted from it, the sound of chanting, the images of strange gods it bore all told me that it came from one of the great temples which dominated the city. A man with a shaven head stood on the passenger deck; he was dressed in a simple white kilt but his air of quiet authority told me that he was a man of consequence.

With some clever oar work his rowers brought the stern of his barge almost even with the deck where Helen and I stood watching, so that the man faced us across a narrow strip of water, and was able to speak to us without raising his voice. When he did speak I almost jumped out of my skin for he said simply, "Menelaus of Sparta, you and your Lady are bidden to the Temple of Isis. This is the summons that Proteus spoke of on the island which Egyptians call Pharos."

Without waiting for any reply he gestured to his servants and they ran out a gangplank from their deck so that it reached the side of our ship; by merely stepping up to it we could walk aboard the barge.

I turned to Helen and she said in that voice so quiet that only I could hear. "We have no choice, Menelaus. The one who spoke to us is not a mortal, nor does he belong to this place. He is an Olympian or a servant of the Olympians."

I took a deep breath and gave orders to Merionathes, my second in command, in as calm a voice as I could manage.

He made a wry face and said, "I don't like it, but I suppose you and the Queen know what you're doing. If you need us, use the signal we used at Troy; set fire to something and we'll fight our way to you."

"We're going to the Temple of Isis," I said. "If that starts to bum you can come after us. Otherwise stay here, or you'll find yourself fighting to get to some burning inn where a drunken sailor has knocked over the brazier." Then I turned and with Helen beside me I stepped onto the gangplank and walked over to the barge.

The shaven-headed man—if he was a man—said nothing to us as the oarsmen impelled us toward the shore. We landed in a green parklike area that was probably part of the temple precincts. A litter waited there for Helen, but she waved it aside, and walked by my side up a tree-bordered path to a massive building that showed no lights at all. But when the shaven-headed man threw open a massive door and gestured for us to enter, I could see that the interior of the great hall into which the door opened was as bright as day; so bright that the evening dusk around us seemed to grow darker.

We stepped into a great hall surrounded by massive pillars: the light came from great white globes suspended from the ceiling by golden chains. At first I thought that the immense room was empty, then I saw a tall woman in dark garments standing across the room from us. As we walked closer to her I saw her face more clearly; it was neither young nor old, Danaan or Egyptian. Perhaps it was not a human face at all: even if I had dared to speak I would not have asked Helen if this was a mortal woman; I did not want to know.

"Welcome, Menelaus of Sparta," the woman said. While I was still wondering why she did not greet Helen the woman fixed her brilliant black eyes on me and said, "Who is the woman with you?" I was first bewildered, then I began to be angry. What were they playing at? If these were Olympians surely they knew who Helen was. If they were not, what was this all about? I tried to keep my voice courteous as I said, "This is Helen of Sparta, my wife and my queen."

The strange woman's eyes seemed to bore into mine and her voice was strangely urgent as she said, "Are you sure, Menelaus? Did you recognize her when you first saw her? Is not Helen of Sparta a daughter of Zeus, with an imperishable beauty that nothing can take away? Do you think that the Powers would permit her to be carried away and subjected to the will of a man who was not her husband? Look, Menelaus, and judge!"

She stepped to a small curtained door on the wall behind her, pulled aside the curtain and stood aside. And through that door there walked... Helen! Helen as she had been on that fateful day when I had left her and our houseguest Paris, Prince of Troy, at the palace in Sparta and gone to Crete for the funeral of my mother's father. Helen in all her dazzling beauty, a beauty so great that you could stand feasting your eyes on it and hardly be aware that time was passing. My heart pounded and I could feel sweat breaking out on my face: I felt as awkward, as dazzled, as I had on the day when unbelievable good fortune had struck and Helen had chosen me out of all her suitors to be her husband.

Now the vision was speaking, and the voice too was just as I remembered it, yet softer, more submissive, without that little note of unshakeable assurance that had sometimes troubled me. "Oh, Menelaus, my husband and my lord," she said, "I am your true wife, your Helen. When Paris stole me away, the gods sent a great wind to blow him here to Egypt. I was brought here to the Temple. Paris was given a false Helen, an illusion whom he took to Troy to be subject to his lust. But I have never been any other man's, but have always belonged to you alone. Here I have waited for you while you performed heroic deeds at Troy. Now all you have to do is claim me, dismiss the false Helen beside you, and carry me back to Sparta in triumph!"

Chapter Seven

THE TRUE HELEN

As she spoke there rushed into my mind all of the things which Proteus had said, words which had then seemed so mysterious. "The Olympians have something waiting for you in Egypt.... accept what the gods have waiting for you there. The choice you make will determine what your future will be." I remembered my first conviction that the woman who waited with Aethra and M'pha could not be Helen, that there must be some mistake.

I turned to face the woman beside me. There was no beauty to dazzle me there though the brisk breeze on the barge from the ship had whipped color into her cheeks just as when she had driven the chariot after Ajax. There was a bruise on her cheek where a stone had been pushed into her face when we hid beneath the seals. Her gaze was steady, and I knew that I would never hear in her voice that sweetly submissive note. She was her own woman, she would never be my possession. She was not mine alone, for ten years she had been the wife of Paris. She did not speak, but only looked at me steadily, calmly. She would not plead or weep or justify; she waited.

I took her hand in mine; it was a little roughened by things she had been doing of late. I smiled at her and the smile she gave me in return showed me a beauty of a different kind than that of the vision which stood before us.

I turned to that vision and said as respectfully as I could, "Why Lady, it is not for me to say that what you say is false. But this I know. This woman beside me is my true wife, the woman I will end my days with, whether they end here and now or long years from now in Sparta or wherever we may go together. Perhaps when I married, I married for little more than what I see before me now in your face and semblance. But even then, I hope, I knew a little of the woman behind the face. And that woman is beside me now. Whether or not she is the true Helen, she is my Helen."

The face before me changed; it was still as dazzlingly beautiful as before, but it no longer looked like the remembered face of Helen. There was anger on that face, but a kind of grudging respect too. "You're a fool," she said, "as great a fool as she is. You deserve each other. Or perhaps... perhaps you're only afraid. Tell me, Menelaus, do you prefer her as she was when you found her or... this way!"

I turned from her to Helen and saw again the face of my memories and my dreams, but this time there was a glint in the eyes and a grim little smile on her lips that told me that behind that beauty was the delightful but formidable woman I loved. "Have you done playing games. Aphrodite?" she asked. I looked at the figure before us and tried to realize that this was a goddess, an immortal who could bless, or blast us.

"Shall I leave it up to you, Helen?" asked the Olympian. "Will you be beautiful or ugly, or perhaps one thing in private and another in public? Which would you prefer, Menelaus?"

"Why, if it is up to Helen," I replied, "let it be up to her. Let her put on beauty or take it off when she wills, like any other adornment. It is not for her adornments I love her."

Again there was that look of grudging respect on Aphrodite's face. "Very well!" she said with a little laugh. "Let it be so; Her loss of beauty was always an illusion anyway: I'll let her control the illusion. You'll need a focus for the power, Helen. Use that mirror of yours. The longer you look in the silver side the plainer you'll get, the longer you look in the golden the more beautiful you'll be. Suit yourself."

Helen laughed a clear, merry trill. "My Lady Aphrodite," she said, "you are . . . yourself. There is no one like you. I accept your gift with thanks; it's one any woman would appreciate, to look just as beautiful as you want to look. But I've had a better gift than that tonight—not your love, Menelaus, I know I've had that for longer than I deserve. What you gave me tonight is a declaration of that love, one I'll always treasure. Thank you, my love. And thank you, my Lady." If the first and last words of that speech were a little ironical, Aphrodite did not seem to notice; she nodded graciously and turned to the dark woman.

She too was now ablaze with a beauty and a power to rival that of Aphrodite, but somehow I did not fear her as I had thought I would fear an Olympian. She smiled at me in a curiously intimate way and said quietly, "Well, Aphrodite, I think that a wiser judge than Paris has made a judgment between your gifts and mine. Menelaus, I am Hera, wife of Zeus, and it is my charge to foster the kind of love between husband and wife that you have shown for Helen. You and Helen are under my protection now, and though I must yield to my old ally, Athena, and let her keep the Argives from their homes a while longer, your wanderings will be both pleasant and prosperous and Hermione will be under my special care."

She turned to Helen. "Child, I am pleased with you," she said. "The promise Aphrodite won from my husband is yours to claim if you choose. Immortality is not for everyone but it is yours to claim if you choose it. Menelaus has the blood of my son Hephaestus in his veins; he can live in the Bright Land if you and he choose to do so."

I had thought that after everything that had happened that night nothing else could surprise me, but this left me gaping. Olympian blood... me? Hephaestus, the smith of the gods? "I've wondered a little sometimes," said Helen with a little grin. "Not just the red hair, though there's none of that in the line of Atreus. And he was always very unlike either Atreus or Agamemnon. But most of all a kind of strength. I was still half in love with Theseus when I married you, Menelaus. I'm sorry that we couldn't have had a better start. Perhaps I didn't really know why I chose you then, but I'm very glad I did."

I smiled at her and took her hand as we turned to leave the presence of the Immortals. If we chose to accept Hera's offer I'd made an odd sort of demigod, but Helen would be as good a goddess as anyone could ask for. However, it was not as a goddess that I loved her, but as Helen; my friend, my lover, my wife.

About the Author

Richard Purtill is Professor Emeritus of Philosophy at Western Washington University, and the author of twenty published books, including The Kaphtu Trilogy, published by 1st Books, *J.R.R. Tolkien: Myth, Morality and Religion*, and *C.S. Lewis's Case for the Christian Faith*. He has made more than twenty visits to Greece, and lived several years in England. His stories have been published in The Magazine of Fantasy and Science Fiction, Isaac Asimov's Science Fiction Magazine, Marion Zimmer Bradley's Fantasy Magazine, Alfred Hitchcock's Mystery Magazine, and The Year's Best Fantasy Stories.

He is a popular presenter at conferences and conventions, and has been guest of honor at Mythcon in San Diego. He is a member of Science Fiction and Fantasy Writers of America, the Author's Guild, and the National Writer's Union. For more information, please visit Richard Purtill's official site at: http://www.alivingdog.com.

Printed in the United States
20286LVS00001B/154

9 781414 055947